ABOUT THE EDITORS

Chiara Bariviera studied classical archeology and worked at La Sapienza University of Rome on research projects in Rome, Pompeii, and Veii. Her studies center on Roman topography and the development of urban landscapes, with a special interest in public architecture and the reconstruction of monumental complexes. She contributed chapters on the Augustan regions Circus Maximus and Piscina Publica for the *Atlas of Ancient Rome*, A. Carandini, ed. (2017). With Pamela O. Long she translated the sixteenth-century Latin treatise on the restoration of the Roman aqueduct *Acqua Vergine* by Agostino Steuco (2015).

☰

Pamela O. Long is a historian of late medieval and early modern European science and technology, and cultural history. Her fellowships include those from American Academy in Rome, the Guggenheim Foundation, the John D. and Catherine T. MacArthur Foundation, and the Institute for Advanced Study at Princeton. Her books include *Openness, Secrecy, Authorship: Technical Arts and the Culture of Knowledge from Antiquity to the Renaissance* (2001); *Artisan/Practitioners and the Rise of the New Sciences* (2011); and *Engineering the Eternal City: Infrastructure, Topography, and the Culture of Knowledge in Late Sixteenth-Century Rome* (2018).

☰

William L. North is Professor of History and Co-Director of Medieval and Renaissance Studies at Carleton College, Northfield, MN. He has published articles on intellectual, religious, and cultural history of medieval Europe from the tenth to the thirteenth centuries and early modern intellectual history, as well as translations of medieval documents from Latin into English. He has served as editor or associate editor of the *Haskins Society Journal* since 2006. His fellowships include those from the American Academy in Rome, Dumbarton Oaks, and the National Endowment for the Humanities.

☰ ☰

☰

THE FLOODS OF THE TIBER

≋

LUIS GÓMEZ

De prodigiosis Tyberis
Inundationibus
ab orbe cõdito ad annũ
M . D . X X X I.
Cõmentarii, Reuereñ.
D . Ludouici Comesii:
Sacri Palatii causarum
Auditoris: ac Viri un-
decunq; doctissimi.

ROMA

THE FLOODS OF THE TIBER

≈

LUIS GÓMEZ

with
Additional Documents on
the Tiber Flood of 1530

Translated by
Chiara Bariviera, Pamela O. Long
&
William L. North

ITALICA PRESS
NEW YORK & BRISTOL
2023

ITALICA PRESS, INC.
99 Wall Street, Suite 650
New York, New York 10005
inquiries@italicapress.com

Library of Congress Cataloging-in-Publication Data
Names: Gomez, Luis, -1542, author. | Bariviera, Chiara, 1976- translator. |
  Long, Pamela O., translator. | North, William L., 1967- translator.
Title: The floods of the Tiber, with additional documents on the Tiber
  flood of 1530 / Luis Gómez ; translated by Chiara Bariviera, Pamela O. Long &
  William L. North.
Other titles: De prodigiosis Tyberis Inundationibus. English
Description: New York ; Bristol : Italica Press, 2023. | Series: Medieval
  and Renaissance texts | Includes bibliographical references and index. |
  Summary: "The first English translation of Luis Gómez's Latin treatise
  (1531) on the flooding of the Tiber River, including a history of the
  river and its floods and a discussion of their consequences. It
  represents a humanist response to dramatic and traumatic environmental
  catastrophe"-- Provided by publisher.
Identifiers: LCCN 2023018112 (print) | LCCN 2023018113 (ebook) | ISBN
  9781599104522 (hardcover) | ISBN 9781599104539 (trade paperback) | ISBN
  9781599104546 (kindle edition) | ISBN 9781599104553 (adobe pdf)
Subjects: LCSH: Floods--Italy--Tiber River--History. |
  Floods--Italy--Rome--History. | Tiber River (Italy)--History. | Tiber
  River Valley (Italy)--History. | Rome (Italy)--History.
Classification: LCC DG69 .G5913 2023 (print) | LCC DG69 (ebook) | DDC
  363.34/930937--dc23/eng/20230427
LC record available at https://lccn.loc.gov/2023018112
LC ebook record available at https://lccn.loc.gov/2023018113

CONTENTS

ACKNOWLEDGEMENTS

The origins of this project about an environmental crisis — the flooding of the Tiber — that struck the city of Rome in 1530 began amid a global health crisis in the spring of 2020: the Covid-19 pandemic. Although separated geographically from each other and often without the possibility of using library collections in the usual ways, we were able to undertake and complete this translation, transcription, and annotation thanks to the research and communication made possible through technological developments like Zoom and the world of resources that have been digitized by libraries around the world and by Google Books. We have been the beneficiaries of decades of development in these areas, and we acknowledge our debt to those who have developed and maintain these vital tools of research, communication, and collaboration.

In addition, we would like to thank the staff at the Library of Congress and Brenda Hellen, head of Interlibrary Loan Services at the Gould Library at Carleton College, for procuring needed materials efficiently amidst the challenging circumstances of the pandemic. Ronald Musto's and Eileen Gardiner's enthusiasm for the project and critical feedback on the manuscript gave us vital encouragement and new insights that improved the work considerably. Finally, we would like to acknowledge and thank Craig Martin, Bob Korn, and Victoria Morse for the myriad kinds of support and encouragement they provided to us throughout our collaboration.

DEDICATION
For
Craig Martin
Bob Korn
and
Victoria Morse
☙

ILLUSTRATIONS

ABBREVIATIONS

CIL
Corpus Inscriptionum Latinarum. Berlin: G. Rimerum, 1862–. Online at: https://cil.bbaw.de.

DBI
Dizionario biografico degli italiani. 100 vols. Rome: Istituto della Enciclopedia Italiana, 1960–2020. Online at: https://www.treccani.it/enciclopedia/ elenco-opere/Dizionario_Biografico.

LTUR
Lexicon topographicum urbis Romae. Eva Margareta Steinby, ed. 6 vols. Rome: Edizioni Quasar, 1993–2000.

MGH
Monumenta Germaniae Historica.

PL
Patrologiae Cursus Completus. Series Latina. 221 vols. J.-P. Migne, ed. Paris: J.-P. Migne, 1844–64.

RIS
Rerum Italicarum Scriptores. 34 volumes. Città di Castello: I Lapi, 1900–1917; Bologna: Zanichelli, 1917–75.

Classical sources are cited using the abbreviations of *The Oxford Classical Dictionary.* 4th ed. Anthony Spawforth and Esther Eidinow, ed. Oxford: Oxford University Press, 2012.

≋ ≋

≋

INTRODUCTION

With the emergence of environmental history and environmental studies in the twentieth century, scholars have investigated with increasing depth and creativity the interactions between humans and the natural world regionally and globally, in urban and rural settings, in normal conditions and in times of catastrophe. Indeed, the new field of disaster studies seeks to understand natural disasters throughout history, investigating not only the natural conditions and context that created them but also the reactions and understandings of the people directly affected.[1] Historical volcanic eruptions, earthquakes, tsunamis, hurricanes, and tornadoes have all received significant study in the last decades, as has flooding in specific geographical areas in modern times. Yet, because of the limited and often laconic nature of the surviving evidence and the challenges of language, flooding in the premodern world has received less attention from environmental historians than its occurrence would merit. Likewise, environmental events have often remained outside the field of view of political, social, and cultural historians.

The increasingly common and catastrophic flooding events in our own era of global warming, however, are leading to change, as people seek deeper and more nuanced understandings of how different communities around the world have confronted environmental emergencies practically and coped with them culturally and psychologically. The fascinating and little-studied source that we present here in translation, the treatise on Tiber River flooding by Luis Gómez, offers the reader not only a vivid, detailed account and causal analysis of the disastrous Roman flood of 1530 but also an opportunity to follow an eyewitness and participant as he seeks to deal with his own personal trauma of the Roman flood disaster through humanist and historical investigation.

---

1. See for example, Andrea Janku, Gerrit J. Schenk, and Franz Mauelshagen, ed., *Historical Disasters in Context: Science, Religion, and Politics* (New York: Routledge, 2012); and Ovanes Akopyan and David Rosenthal, ed., *Disaster in the Early Modern World: Examinations, Representations, Interventions* (Abingdon: Routledge, forthcoming).

Fig. 1. *View of Ponte Fabricio at Tiber Island with two mills. Hieronymus Cock, "Pontis nunc 'Quatuor Capitum' olim Fabricii prospectis," Etching,* 1550/51. *Courtesy of the Rijksmuseum, Amsterdam.*

The Tiber River winds through the center of the city of Rome in central Italy. In the sixteenth century, the river was fundamental to the life of the city, providing it with a water supply for drinking, washing, and industrial uses, as well as local fishing. Its rapid current powered the city's grain mills, which ground the flour that was the basis of the urban food supply [Fig. 1]. It was also the depository for tons of sewage and other refuse that the city generated every day. Yet, just as the river supported the life of the city, it also threatened it. Since antiquity and throughout the Middle Ages, the Tiber flooded periodically, often with devastating consequences. Thus, in the sixteenth century, with the city's growing population clustered in the low-lying flood plain near the riverbanks and the severity of flooding increasing due to climate change, the flooding of the Tiber became a catastrophic event.[2] This was the

2.   For the Tiber River and its flooding, see Gregory S. Aldrete, *Floods of the Tiber in Ancient Rome* (Baltimore: Johns Hopkins University Press, 2007); Elisa Andretta, "Les médecins du Tibre: La construction d'un savoir sur les fleuves dans la Rome du 16e siècle," *Histoire, Médecine et Santé* 11 (2017): 99–129; Mauro Bencivenga, Eugenio Di Loreto, and Lorenzo Liperi, "Piene storiche del Tevere a Roma," *L'Acqua* 3 (1999): 17–24; Pio Bersani and Mauro Bencivenga, *Le piene del Tevere a Roma dal V secolo a.C. all'anno 2000* (Rome: Servizio Idrografico e Mareografico Nazionale, 2010); Vittorio Di Martino, Roswitha Di Martino, and Massimo Belati, *Huc Tiber Ascendit: Le memorie delle inondazioni del Tevere a Roma* (Rome: Arbor Sapientiae, 2017), 7–66 and 83–89; Cesare D'Onofrio, *Il Tevere: L'Isola Tiberina, le inondazioni, i molini, i porti, le rive, i muraglioni, i ponti di Roma* (Rome: Romana Società Editrice, 1980), 301–30; Silvia Enzi, "Le inondazioni del Tevere a Roma tra il XVI e XVIII secolo nelle fonti bibliotecarie del tempo," in *Mélanges de l'École française de Rome, Italie et Méditerranée* 118.1 (2006): 13–20; Anna Esposito, "Il Tevere e Roma," in *La calamità ambientali nel tardo Medioevo europeo: Realtà, percezioni, reazioni*, Michael Matheus, et al., ed. (Florence: Firenze University Press, 2010), 257–75; idem, "Le inondazioni del Tevere tra tardo Medioevo e prima età moderna: Leggende, racconti, testimonianze," *Mélanges de l'École française de Rome, Italie et Méditerranée* 118.1 (2006): 7–12; Pietro Frosini, *Il Tevere: Le inondazioni di Roma e i provvedimenti presi dal governo italiano per evitarle* (Rome: Accademia Nazionale dei Lincei, 1977), 129–233; Pamela O. Long, *Engineering the Eternal City: Infrastructure, Topography, and the Culture of Knowledge in Late Sixteenth-Century Rome* (Chicago: University

case on October 8, 1530, during which the floodwaters reached 18.95 masl (meters above sea level).[3]

Flooding in the sixteenth century was a problem not only in Rome but in many other locales in Europe. Although flooding is always a possibility on all rivers, the cooling that came with Europe's Little Ice Age increased both the number of floods and their severity.[4] In many cities, including Rome, a burgeoning population and the increased construction of houses and other kinds of buildings on the flood plain made the effects of flooding more serious — more people and animals were drowned, and more buildings were destroyed. In Rome, precisely because of the legacy of advanced sewage and water infrastructure, floods were particularly damaging because flood conditions caused river water to flow up the sewers and other conduits, spreading their fetid material throughout the city. This, along with the numerous carcasses of dead animals, polluted wells, and made clean water scarce. Disease naturally followed floods, as

of Chicago Press, 2018), 19–41; idem, "Responses to a Recurrent Disaster: Flood Writings in Rome, 1476–1606," in Akopyan and Rosenthal, *Disaster*; Annalisa Marsico, *Il Tevere e Roma nell'alto medioevo: Alcuni aspetti del rapporto tra il fiume e la città* (Rome: Società alla Biblioteca Vallicelliana, 2018), 98–107 (for the mills); and Maria Margarita Segarra Lagunes, *Il Tevere e Roma: Storia di una simbiosi* (Rome: Gangemi, 2004), 69–133. More generally, see Lydia Barnett, *After the Flood: Imagining the Global Environment in Early Modern Europe* (Baltimore: Johns Hopkins University Press, 2019); and Katherine Wentworth Rinne, *The Waters of Rome: Aqueducts, Fountains, and the Birth of the Baroque City* (New Haven: Yale University Press, 2010).

3.   Aldrete, *Floods,* 244, for the masl. See also Di Martino, Di Martino, and Belati, *Huc Tiber Ascendit,* 62–65; Anna Esposito, "Roma e i suoi diluvi," in Giuliano Dati, *Del diluvio de Roma del MCCCCXCV a dì IIII de decembre,* Anna Esposito and Paola Farenga, ed. (Rome: Roma nel Rinascimento, 2011), 5–26, esp. 22–26; and Frosini, *Il Tevere,* 160–65.

4.   For the Little Ice Age, see John Aberth, *An Environmental History of the Middle Ages: The Crucible of Nature* (London: Routledge, 2013), 49–51; Brian Fagan, *The Little Ice Age: How Climate Made History, 1300–1850* (New York: Basic Books, 2000); and for the global picture, Jean M. Grove, *Little Ice Ages: Ancient and Modern* 1, 2nd ed. (London: Routledge, 2004), esp. 564–90.

Gómez noted. In Rome in 1530, hunger did as well, since the mills for grinding grain into flour for bread were all river mills (located in the Tiber and powered by the river current). Flooding thus deprived Romans of even the most basic necessities: bread and water.

With regard to the built environment, river floods were especially threatening to bridges. In modern terminology, the main reason bridges fail is because of a process known as "scour." In this process, a rapidly moving river removes material from the riverbed around the piers or other bridge supports, creating holes that, in turn, undermine the entire bridge. Because bridges narrow the water channel and thus tend to create eddies, they intensify scouring, ironically accelerating their own demise. Bridges are also threatened by debris crashing against them, a common occurrence during floods, when uprooted trees, parts of buildings, and other rubble are swept rapidly downstream. Such debris could not only damage bridges through their impact but also through the increased water pressure that these accidental dams generated. Finally, situated on a floodplain, Rome was more generally vulnerable to the natural tendency of rivers to alter their courses within the floodplain, and at no time more than during a flood.[5] Gómez and his contemporaries would not have framed the problems of bridges during floods the way modern civil engineers do. But he was in fact aware of and discussed each one of these issues.

THE AUTHOR

Luis Gómez was born c.1482 in Orihuela, Valencia. After his initial studies close to home, he pursued the study of civil and canon law at the University of Bologna before moving to Padua to take up a teaching position by 1522. There he is known to have lectured on the *Institutes* of Justinian as well as canon law. By 1528, he was serving at the papal court in Rome as an auditor of the Rota, that is, a judge in one of the papal tribunals called the Sacra Romana Rota. He then became director of the Penitenzieria Apostolica (the Apostolic Penitentiary), which was a papal tribunal with jurisdiction over such matters as the issue of indulgences and absolutions from

---

5. Les Hamill, *Bridge Hydraulics* (Boca Raton: CRC Press, 1999), esp. 9–23, 61–102.

excommunications. In 1534, he was made bishop of Sarno, located east of Naples. As attested in an epigraph from a church in Orihuela, he died in 1542 in the city of Macerata in the Marches and was buried in its cathedral.[6]

Gómez was an accomplished jurist whose works focused primarily on canon law and more specifically on legal and administrative issues arising from the activity of the Sacra Rota.[7] Indeed, his was one the significant voices in the development of administrative canon law in the sixteenth century. In addition to his training in the law, he seems to have shared the interests of his humanist contemporaries in classical texts and *realia*. His wide-ranging citations and close readings attest to his being very well-read in classical and medieval sources on Roman history. He seems also to have kept current with the medical literature and the humanist scholarship of his own day.

Gómez's treatise on the 1530 flooding of the Tiber, *De prodigiosis Tyberis Inundationibus ab orbe condito ad annum MDXXXI Commentarii*, represents a literary and scholarly departure. Clearly motivated and informed by his own experience of the flood, it is distinctly different in aim, method, and tone from his other writings. At the same time, it bears eloquent witness to how he

---

6.   Gómez is also cited as Ludovico Comesius, or Gomesius. His death date is variously given as 1542, 1543, and 1553; but 1542 is the correct date. Biographical entries on Gómez can be found in a large microfiche biographical collection with index: Victor Herrero Mediavilla, ed., *Indice Biográfico de España, Portugal e Iberoamérica* (ADEPI), 4th ed., 7 vols. (Munich: K.G. Saur, 2007), 3, s.v., referring to Part I, microfiche 393, frames 327–36; and Part II, microfiche 400, frames 352–61 (epitaph on frame 329). See also Juan Beneyto, "Luis Gómez, jurista de Orihuela," *Anales del Centro de Cultura Valenciana*, 2d ser. 20 (1952): 192–95; Joseph Folliet, "Gómez Louis," in *Dictionnaire de droit canonique*, Raoul Naz, ed. (Paris: Librairie Letouzey et Ané, 1953), 5, cols. 974–75; and A. García y García, "Gómez, Luis," in *Diccionario de Historia Eclesiástica de España* (Madrid: Instituto Enrique Flores, 1972), 2:1026.

7.   For a discussion of Gómez's legal writings and thought, see Silvia Di Paolo, "Da *regulae* particolari a norme generali: Verso un diritto amministrativo della Chiesa (XV–XVI sec.)," *Historia et Ius* 11 (2017): paper 6, esp. 9–13; online at www.historiaetius.eu.

used his critical methods and wide scholarly learning to cope with a personal and community crisis. In each of the three sections of the resulting treatise, the reader watches Gómez extract from highly varied sources small details, often mentioned in passing, that relate to his theme. The text thus reveals a highly discriminating method of reading across a wide range of materials. It also bears witness to the way in which Rome's history and antiquities themselves were central concerns for members of the Curia and to the fact that Gómez, although not known for his humanist or antiquarian interests, was nonetheless part of these circles and shared their interest in and complex awareness of the city of Rome as both a human and a built space.

The flood of 1530 was a catastrophic event for Romans and others who lived in the city. It was also a bitter sequel to the traumatic Sack of Rome that had occurred three years before in May 1527. An ongoing conflict between the papacy and its allies and the forces of the Holy Roman Emperor Charles V (r.1500–58) led, eventually, to Rome being besieged by an army of German and Spanish troops under the command of Charles III, duke of Bourbon (1490–1527). Unfortunately, when Charles "the Bourbon," as he was called, was killed in the initial attack on the city, leaderless soldiers — who had not been paid for months — looted, burned, kidnapped, raped, castrated, and murdered in a rampage that had lasted for ten long months. The physical city was devastated, its people decimated or dispersed, and Pope Clement VII was taken captive.[8]

---

8.   The large literature on the Sack includes E.W. Chamberlain, *The Sack of Rome* (New York: Dorset, 1979); André Chastel, *The Sack of Rome, 1527*, Beth Archer, trans. (Princeton, NJ: Princeton University Press, 1983); Kenneth Gouwens, *Remembering the Renaissance: Humanist Narratives of the Sack of Rome* (Leiden: Brill, 1998); Judith Hook, *The Sack of Rome, 1527* (London: Macmillan, 1972); Massimo Miglio et al., ed., *Il sacco di Roma del 1527 e l'immaginario collettivo* (Rome: Istituto Nazionale di Studi Romani, 1986); Giulia Ponsiglione, *La "ruina" di Roma: Il sacco del 1527 e la memoria letteraria* (Rome: Carocci, 2010); and Manfredo Tafuri, "*Roma coda mundi:* The Sack of Rome: Rupture and Continuity," in Tafuri, *Interpreting the Renaissance: Princes, Cities, Architects*, Daniel Sherer, trans. (New Haven: Yale University Press and Cambridge, MA: Harvard University Graduate School of Design, 2006), 157-159. For a detailed contemporary account of

Romans were just beginning to recover from that long trauma (to which Gómez several times alludes), when on October 8, 1530, the Tiber River began its own course of devastation. This flood was — both in the memory of the victims and in fact — one of the worst that the city had experienced. As had writers describing the Sack, who looked to past sackings of Rome to understand their present moment, Gómez believed that his account of previous floods might offer the solace of historical perspective to traumatized victims, allowing them to feel a connection to their ancestors, who had experienced similar events, as well as the hope that they, too, would survive and rebuild. Whether he succeeded in this purpose or not, Gómez's treatise is the earliest work dedicated wholly to Tiber River flooding. His careful assemblage of information about the river's floods from ancient times made it the starting point for future studies, and later writers on the Tiber and its flooding — especially those dealing with the floods of 1557 and 1598 — drew on it extensively.[9]

For the modern scholar, Gómez's treatise offers a similarly rich array of information and insights. It provides an eyewitness account of a major environmental disaster affecting one of the most developed urban landscapes in Europe and shows how contemporaries analyzed the causes and consequences of natural disasters. It also offers a rich and varied example of how contemporary scholars could mobilize their written sources; exercise skills in reading and historical interpretation honed by their studies in law, medicine, and the classics; and use the past to make sense of and critique their present and reimagine the future. As

---

the event, see Luigi Guicciardini, *The Sack of Rome,* James H. McGregor, trans. (New York: Italica Press, 1993).

9.   Gómez's treatise was notably used in the physician Andrea Bacci's treatise written after the 1557 Tiber flood, *Del Tevere: Della natura et bonta dell'acque & delle inondationi Libri II* (Rome: Vincenzo Luchino, 1558); and revised as Bacci, *Del Tevere [...] libri tre [...]* (Venice: Aldus, 1576). In a further revision after the flood of 1598, Bacci translated and summarized Gómez's treatise in Italian to become book 4 of his 1599 version of that treatise: *Del Tevere dell'eccell. dottore medico e filosofo Andrea Baccio libro quarto* (Rome: Stampatori Camerali, 1599).

we increasingly confront our own environmental challenges, Gómez's work thus offers both method and hope.

THE TREATISE

Following a practice of contemporary authors, Gómez began his treatise on Tiber River flooding with a dedicatory letter, in this case to a fellow Spaniard and potential patron, Cardinal García de Loaysa (1478–1546). He then anchored his project in classical antiquity — and perhaps called for administrative reform in his own day — by publishing a recently unearthed inscription from ancient Rome that named the curators of the Tiber and of its riverbed. The problems of the Tiber and its management had a long history. Echoing Gómez's own tribute, the publisher of the text, Francesco Minizio Calvo (fl.1521–41), included his own dedicatory letter to Cardinal Loaysa. Calvo then saluted the spiritual and political leader of Rome himself, Pope Clement VII (r.1523–34), offering a poem on the flood by the poet Francesco Maria Molza (1489–1544).

Gómez divided the treatise that follows into three parts. The first concerns the Tiber River in general — what the ancients called it, their attitudes toward it, the many references to it in ancient texts, and the presumption in antiquity that the river was divine. In the second part, he seeks to learn whether the flood of his own day was, in fact, the largest and most devastating through reconstructing the history of Tiber flooding from the beginnings of Rome to his own day. To create this chronology of disaster, which ran from 414 BCE to 1530, he gathered information through a meticulous reading of ancient and medieval narratives as well as an analysis of the material evidence from buildings and inscriptions, assembling them into discrete accounts of twenty-two major floods.

He then recounted the twenty-third flood, the flood of his own time and its devastating impact on people and property. Here he drew his information not from textual authorities but from his own vivid experiences and those of his contemporaries. In the third part, Gómez shifts from historical retrospection and description to a more general consideration of the human consequences of flooding, including the ruin and destruction of moveable property, private houses and public buildings, and pestilence. He likewise looked to the future with reflections on mitigation and prevention, foreshadowing a rich vein of inquiry in the decades to come.

Gómez's many references to ancient and medieval texts testify to the fact that his own treatise was dependent on prior sources. However, many of his references are to casual mentions of particular floods or to relatively brief reports. Only in the late fifteenth century did Tiber River flooding receive more extensive treatment. After the flood of 1476 (at 17.32 masl.), the diarists Stefano Infessura (c.1435–1500) and Jacopo Gherardi (1434–1516) each vividly described the catastrophe, mostly focusing on the flood's effect on the pope and his court.[10] The flood of 1476 was also described in detail in three letters, one by Cardinal Ammannati Piccolomini (1422–79), one by Enrico de Ampringen, a secretary in the Roman Curia, and one by Johannes Marchus, a secretary to the duke of Milan. Each letter provided a vivid description of the flood.[11]

10.　For the 1476 flood, see especially Esposito, "Roma e i suoi 'diluvi,'" 13–15; Di Martino, Di Martino, and Belati, *Huc Tiber ascendit*, 48–50; and Frosini, *Il Tevere*, 153–54. For the height of the flood, see Aldrete, *Floods*, 244. For Infessura and Gherardi, see Stefano Infessura, *Diario della città di Roma*, Oreste Tommasini, ed. (Rome: Forzani E.C. Tipografi del Senato, 1890), 80; and Jacopo Gherardi, *Il diario romano di Jacopo Gherardi*, Enrico Carusi, ed., RIS 23.3 (Città di Castello: S. Lapi, 1904), 31. For an astute discussion of both of these figures in another context, see Maren Elisabeth Schwab and Anthony Grafton, *The Art of Discovery: Digging into the Past in Renaissance Europe* (Princeton, NJ: Princeton University Press, 2022), esp. 116–17 and 129–32.

11.　For Piccolomini's letter, which was addressed to Goro Loli-Piccolomini and included an attached poem, see Iacopo Ammannati Piccolomini, *Lettere (1444–1479)*, 3 vols., Paolo Cherubini, ed. (Rome: Ministero per i Beni Culturali e Ambientali and Ufficio Centrale per i Beni Archivistici, 1997), 1:154–56 and 3:2010–14 (Letter 842). For Enrico de Ampringen's letter, see Wilhelm Vischer and Heinrich Boos, ed. "Johannis Knebel capellani ecclesie Basiliensis Diarium," *Basler Chroniken* 2 (1880): 408–9; and Esposito, "Roma e i suoi 'diluvi,'" 13–14. For Marchus' letter, see Johannes Marchus, "Inondazioni a Roma, Venezia e Como nel 1478," *Bollettino Storico della Svizzera Italiana* 6 (1884): 107.

As with the flood of 1476, that of 1495 (16.88 masl.) was also described in detail in two letters. The authors of both are unknown, but each was in Rome at the time of the flood, and each was associated with the Venetian embassy in Rome. One was in the retinue of Girolamo Zorzi (1430–1507), the Venetian ambassador, and addressed his letter to the emperor of the Holy Roman Empire, Maximilian I (r.1486–1519). The second was also associated with the Venetian embassy. Both letters contain detailed, vivid descriptions of the horrors of the flood.[12] However, the most striking written response to the flood of 1495 was the one penned by a Florentine priest, Giovanni Dati (c.1445–1523) who served at the church of San Giovanni in Laterano in Rome and was also a prolific author and translator. Dati wrote a long poem of 109 octaves (eight-line stanzas), concerning the flood of 1495, which he considered a sign of divine retribution. He went through each of the districts (rioni) of Rome describing the damage to buildings (for the most part churches and palaces) and other structures, such as gates.[13]

At 18.95 masl., the flood of 1530 was significantly higher than the previous two floods. Shortly after the catastrophe, two significant reports of the event were penned. The first was in a letter written by Giovanni Battista Sanga (1496–1532), a humanist literary figure and secretary to cardinals and popes. Sanga wrote a riveting description of the catastrophe in a letter sent to Alessandro de' Medici, who would soon become duke of Florence (r.1532–37). A second account of this flood is found in an anonymous treatise printed in Bologna in November 1530.[14]

---

12. For the 1495 flood, see Aldrete, *Floods*, 244, for the masl. See also Di Martino, Di Martino, and Belati, *Huc Tiber Ascendit*, 50–54; Esposito, "Roma e i suoi 'diluvi,'" 15–19; and Frosini, *Il Tevere*, 155–60. For the first letter, see Domenico Malipiero, ed., *Annali Veneti Dall'Anno 1457 al 1500 ordinati e abbreviati dal Senatore Francesco Longo* (Florence: Gio. Pietro Vieusseax, 1848), 409–10, and for the second, 411–15.

13. Giuliano Dati, *Del diluvio de Roma del MCCCCXCV a dì IIII de decembre*, Anna Esposito and Paola Farenga, ed. (Rome: Roma nel Rinascimento, 2011).

14. Sanga's letter is reproduced in Michele Carcani, *Il Tevere: Le sue inondazioni dall'origine di Roma fino ai giorni nostri* (Rome: Tipografia

Gómez's treatise was thus not the first piece of writing about Tiber River flooding, nor was it the first description of the flood of 1530. Nevertheless, his treatise was unique. It was both the first systematic treatise and the first Latin treatise on the topic. We know of no evidence concerning how it was received or read in the immediate aftermath of its publication. We also have no idea how many copies were originally printed. It is now quite rare, though its presence in Google Books makes it delightfully, if deceptively, available. The WorldCat database, for example, lists only seven copies held in libraries worldwide (though more may exist outside this database). In other words, Gómez's work in Latin may initially have had a comparatively limited and local readership.

However, Tiber River flooding continued through the sixteenth century and later, giving Gómez's treatise continued relevance. The floods of 1557 and 1598 were particularly catastrophic. Both prompted writings describing the floods and proposing solutions to the problem. Among them, the most important was the work of the physician Andrea Bacci (1524–1600). In some ways, Bacci's interests differed from those of Gómez. He wrote as a physician and was particularly interested in the medicinal qualities of spring waters in diverse places in Italy, which he believed differed one from the other. He had also written tracts on springs before the flood of 1557. Bacci was one of the strong advocates of the salubrity of Tiber River water in a debate of physicians on the subject, some of whom argued vehemently against the advisability of drinking Tiber water.[15] As a response to the 1557 flood, in 1558 Bacci wrote a treatise in Italian on the Tiber River. He expanded it in 1576, devoting the first two chapters primarily to the quality and potability of various waters

---

Romana, 1875), 45–46. For the Anonymous of Bologna we have used Anonymous, *Diluvio di Roma che fu a VII d'ottobre, l'anno M.D. XXX....* Benvenuto Gasparoni, ed. Arti e Lettere. Scritti Raccolti da Francesco e Benvenuto Gasparoni, 2 vols. (Rome: Tipografia delle Scienze Matematiche e Fisiche, 1865), 2:81–98, 106–31. See Appendix for both documents.

15. On this debate, see Elisa Andretta, "Les médecins du Tibre"; and Giuseppe Bonaccorso, "Roma e le sue acque potabili nel Cinquecento: La competizione con il Tevere," *Roma Moderna e Contemporanea* 17 (2009): 73–90, and n. 45.

including the Tiber's, and only the last chapter to its flooding. Bacci was interested in determining the causes of flooding and increasingly, in subsequent editions of his text, in suggesting solutions. In his final 1599 edition, published a year before his death, he added a fourth book, in which he provided a partial Italian translation and summary of Gómez's treatise, acknowledging that he was publishing the work of a "Monsignor Gomesio." He included Gómez's history of flooding and then added to it with descriptions of the floods of 1557, the two floods of 1589, and the flood of 1598.[16] The absence of any reference to Gómez in either the 1558 or the 1576 editions of his work suggests that Bacci himself may have discovered Gómez's treatise only after 1576.

Bacci participated in the cardinalate *congregazione* (a committee headed by a cardinal) that was created by Pope Clement VIII (r.1592–1605) after the 1598 flood and so must have been acquainted with the obscure poet and writer Giacomo Castiglione (dates unknown). Castiglione wrote his own treatise on Tiber River flooding, also published in 1599, explicitly for the elucidation of that committee. Part of his contribution, Castiglione notes, was to discuss what the "old authors" (*vecchi auctori*) said about the matter. He includes among them Gómez (Comesio), pointing specifically to Gómez's history of flooding from the beginning to the flood of 1530, and noting the "very great diligence" (*grandissima diligenza*) of the author in collecting this information. Although the relationship of Castiglione's treatise to the 1599 version of Bacci's is unclear (both were published in 1599), Castiglione's history of Tiber flooding augments Gómez's for the early centuries as well as in the sixteenth century. In contrast, Bacci makes additions only after the flood of 1530. Castiglione also corrects Gómez

---

16. For Bacci's treatises on Tiber River flooding, see p. 8 n. 9 above; Long, *Engineering the Eternal City*, 25–27 and 36–41; and Nancy G. Siraisi, "*Historiae*: Natural History, Roman Antiquity, and Some Roman Physicians," in *Historia: Empiricism and Erudition in Early Modern Europe*, Gianna Pomata and Nancy G. Siraisi, ed. (Cambridge, MA: MIT Press, 2005), 325–54. For the floods of 1557 and 1598, see Long, *Engineering the Eternal City*, 19–41 (for floods between 1557 and 1589); and Segarra Lagunes, *Il Tevere e Roma*, 69–133 (discussing a number of floods and flood remedies, including the flood of 1598), both with further bibliography.

and expresses surprise that the jurist omitted at least one seemingly important flood.[17]

Despite Bacci's and Castiglione's great attention to Gómez's treatise and their use of it in their own treatises of 1599, we have not found other notice of the 1531 tract in the following centuries. Perhaps this lack of attention signals a change in culture. In place of Gómez's many careful references to ancient authors and his accompanying erudite humanist scholarship, later writers seem to have been far more interested in practical solutions to the perennial problem of Tiber River flooding.

THE TRANSLATION

This translation is the result of a collective effort of three scholars who provided their different expertise, ranging from Roman archeology and topography to late ancient, medieval, and early modern history of science, technology, and cultural history. Our aim was to produce a clear, accurate, and readable English version of the original text — here transcribed in full for the first time — accompanied by an informative introduction, full and accurate annotations, and a comprehensive bibliography.

The entire translating process, which was articulated in multiple phases of individual work and collective revision, was inspired by principles of reliability based on accuracy, consistency, and explicitness. We sought to convey, in the best way possible, the specific style of the original text and respect its formal characteristics, while making it accessible to a modern readership. This process often included rendering long Latin constructions into more comprehensible prose, for example, by dividing a very long sentence into shorter ones and by converting passive into active voice, or transforming some particular Latin constructions, like ablative absolutes, into shorter, independent clauses. The goal was to preserve as much as possible the logical sequence, meaning, and tone of the original, while rendering it into

---

17. Giacomo Castiglione, *Trattato dell'inondatione del Tevere di Iacomo Castiglione Romano* (Rome: Guglielmo Facciotto, 1599), 1–2, for the congregation; 3, 23, 24, 28, 34, and 44 for specific references to Gómez; and 18–45 for his history of Tiber River flooding, primarily based on Gómez's treatise. Thus far we have not been able to discover Castiglione's life dates.

idiomatic English. For accuracy of reference, the number-letter references in brackets throughout the translation and Latin text refer to the 1531 edition's signatures and foliation, thus: []. For readers interested in Gómez's Latin style, we have included here the complete Latin text on pp. 89–122. Throughout the margins of the Latin text we have included the pagination of the English translation.

The annotations that accompany the translation are the product of the translators' different training and provide the historical, topographical, and technical details needed for full understanding. The result is a clear, accurate, and readable text that represents a reliable research tool for scholars, students, and interested readers who want to explore the multifaceted reality of urban and environmental studies in the premodern world.

✲ ✲

✲

Fig. 2. Detail of Fig. 1. *View of Ponte Fabricio at Tiber Island with two mills.*

THE FLOODS OF THE TIBER

Luis Gómez, *Commentaries on the Prodigious Floods of the Tiber from the Founding of Rome to the Year 1531* by the Reverend Lord Luis Gómez, Auditor of Cases at the Sacred Palace and a Most Learned Man in All Respects.[1] [A2r]

> To the very Reverend and Great Father Lord García de Loaysa, Cardinal of the Holy Roman Church,[2] Luis Gómez, Spaniard, Auditor of Cases of the Holy Palace, sends warmest greetings.

Although I found refuge from that Tiber flood in your home, greatest father, as if on Deucalion's ship,[3] and was received here by your people with splendid, manifestly generous, and royal treatment (which you often use to welcome scholars), in my mind I nevertheless lamented the wretched condition of the city. For I had been deprived of the most serious-minded company of the fathers whose daily conversation and exchange of shared interests I often enjoyed in the Curia and in the City. I missed those beautiful duties of the Republic, which, along with my own utmost efforts, could bring me praise and honor. I missed my private studies and my own books, which I normally used to lighten my heaviest cares. Moreover, I saw that everything was dragged down by the Tiber's rage and submerged

---

1.   Rome: Francesco Minizio Calvo, 1531.

2.   García de Loaysa y Mendoza (1478–1546) was a Dominican priest from Toledo (Spain) and master general of the order. He resigned to become bishop of Osma on June 8, 1524. He had a varied and distinguished career in Spain, which included his role as the confessor and close aid to Emperor Charles V. Loaysa was made cardinal on May 16, 1530 but returned to Spain in 1533. See Salvador Miranda, ""Loaysa y Mendozo, O.P., Garcia de (1478–1546)," in *The Cardinals of the Holy Roman Church*, at https://cardinals.fiu.edu/bios1530.htm#Loaysa.

3.   Deucalion, son of Prometheus, along with his wife Pyrrha, survived the flood sent by Zeus to destroy all humanity by building an ark and landing on Mount Parnassus. This myth is recounted in Ovid's *Metamorphoses* (Ov. *Met.* 1. 347–415) and is also mentioned by Aristotle (Arist. *Meteor.* 352a 31–b 4).

beneath the waves. Amidst such great evils of the Republic, I was only able to grieve and despair, until you, greatest father, pillar of men of letters, returned from the Esquiline and lifted my afflicted heart with your very wise words and your very kind manner.

After much discussion back and forth (as happens), our conversation chanced upon the subject of floods. Many experts from your household were present, who contentiously reported certain prodigies of the Tiber. Then, I, who had nothing at that time to lift my spirits, felt a great urge to resume my old studies, from which [A2v] judicial cases had gradually distracted me, and to bring order to certain puzzling aspects of this subject that are perhaps even more "insubstantial" than the Syracusan "trifles."[4] I would privately dedicate them to you, who are otherwise burdened by great cares, in order to relieve my spirits, yet not with the stipulation that they be published. For they are not the kinds of things that merit publication. Nor are they polished with such clarity that they are worthy to be read by experts. Even if they might seem worthy, they have been assembled with such great haste and completed in such a short and calamitous time that — since there was no time for correction — they could not avoid criticism. Be that as it may, you will forgive my eagerness. For, since you yourself have been the author of my boldness, you must acknowledge this offspring that has emerged in an untimely birth. Farewell, glory of scholars, and [continue to] love me as you do.

[A3r] In Rome, outside the doors of San Giovanni Evangelista in the rione of the house of Reverend Lord Tommaso da Prato, a most upstanding datary:[5]

---

4.   On Syracusan trifles, see Arist. *Pol.* 5 1303b.19–30. In this passage Aristotle recalls a Syracusan lovers' dispute that led to changes in the city's constitution to make the point that big changes often have small beginnings.

5.   This refers to the church of San Giovanni in Ajno on via Monserrato, which was the titular church of San Giovanni Evangelista and had "DIVO EVANGE" as part of an inscription on the architrave of the front door. It was in the rione (district) Regola (once Arenula) about two blocks from the house of Tommaso Cortesi da Prato on via di Montoro, previously called vicolo di Corte Savella in the same rione. According to CIL, 6.1237, the inscription mentioned here was found in 1526 in front of his house. It is a Tiber bank marker from the time of Tiberius (r.14–37 CE). See Carlo

CAIUS VIBIUS RUFUS SON OF CAIUS
SEXTUS SOTIDIUS STRABO SON OF SEXTUS
LIBUSCIDIUS
CAIUS CALPESANUS STATIUS RUFUS SON OF CAIUS
MARCUS CLAUDIUS MARCELLUS, SON OF MARCUS
LUCIUS VISELLIUS VARRO SON OF CAIUS
CURATORS OF THE TIBER'S RIVERBANKS AND RIVERBED
BY THE FINAL DECREE OF THE SENATE SET THIS
BOUNDARY.[6]

⅏

Pietrangeli, *Guide Rionali di Roma: Rione VII – Regola*, pt. 2 (Rome: Fratelli Palombi, 1984), 26–28. For Tommaso Cortesi da Prato (c.1470–1543), see Franca Petrucci, "Cortesi, Tommaso," DBI 29 (1983): 772–73. He is listed in the 1527 census as living in Regola. See Egmont Lee, ed., *Habitatores in Urbe: The Population of Renaissance Rome / La popolazione di Roma nel Rinascimento* (Rome: Casa Editrice Università La Sapienza, 2006), 235 (no. 5695). There is a discrepancy between the inscription's location as reported in Gómez (1531) and the find spot reported in the CIL (1526). The area is the same, and it is notable that the Sack of Rome occurred between the two references, which may have caused items to be moved. It is also known that Cortesi fled Rome during the Sack, leaving in such haste that family members, including a son, were left behind.

6.   The identities of these individuals are as follows: (1) Caius Vibius Rufus was a Roman senator, suffect consul in 16 CE under the reign of Emperor Tiberius. See Alison E. Cooley, *The Cambridge Manual of Latin Epigraphy* (Cambridge: Cambridge University Press, 2012), 459. (2) Sextus Sotidius Strabo Libuscidianus (i.e., son of Libuscidius) was also governor of Galatia in 20 CE and the author of an edict on transportation in the territory of the city of Sagalassos (Turkey). See Andrea Zuccaro, "Alcune osservazioni storiche e lessicali sull'editto del legato tiberiano Sotidius Libuscidianus (AE 1976, 653)," *Studi Classici e Orientali* 65.1 (2019): 245–75 at 245. (3) The name of Caius Calpesanus Statius Rufus is mentioned only in one other inscription, which lists the *curatores locorum publicorum iudicandorum* (CIL 6.1266). (4) Marcus Claudius Marcellus is only known through his father of the same name (42–23 BCE) who was the nephew of Emperor Augustus and a famous military commander. (5) Lucius Visellius Varro was a Roman senator, consul in 24 CE. See Cooley, *Cambridge Manual*, 459. CIL 6.1237 = *Inscriptiones Latinae Selectae* 5925.

[A3v] To the very Reverend and Illustrious Lord Don García de Loaysa y Mendoza, Cardinal of Osma,[7] Francesco Minizio Calvo[8] sends greetings.

Greatest lord, I cannot help but give you very special thanks in my name and indeed in the name of all scholars, because you wanted this little book on Tiber floods to be printed and published by me. It was written in a most learned and sagacious manner by Luis Gómez, an outstanding man of the highest erudition. All scholars shall confess – even more than I, by Hercules – that they owe you a debt because they have received this at your instigation from that reluctant author who had dedicated these commentaries to you alone. For you have shown yourself not only to be extremely kind in this matter but also to help all scholars as much as you can and to warmly support them in no modest way. You shine brilliantly among the other cardinals of the Christian Republic. You are praised for all your most excellent virtues and noble qualities of mind. In the eyes of Clement VII, pontifex maximus and Caesar [r.1523–34], you have greater authority than anyone else at this time.[9] Indeed, what could have been a source of erudition and no small delight for you alone, you have given me

7.   For García de Loaysa y Mendoza, see p. 17 n. 2.

8.   Francesco Minizio Calvo from Como in northern Italy was active as a publisher and printer in Rome between 1521 and 1531. He sold books in his shop in the rione Parione. He is listed in the census of 1527 as "*estampatore*." See Fernanda Ascarelli, *La tipografia cinquecentina italiana* (Florence: Sansoni Antiquariato, 1953), 66; Francesco Barberi, "Le edizioni romane di Francesco Minizio Calvo," in *Miscellanea di scritti di bibliografia ed erudizione in memoria di Luigi Ferrari* (Florence: L.S. Olschki, 1952), 57–97, esp. 57–64 and 92–93; and Christopher L.C.E. Witcombe, *Print Publishing in Sixteenth-Century Rome: Growth and Expansion, Rivalry and Murder* (London: Harvey Miller, 2008), 9, 66. For the 1527 census listing, see Lee, Habitatores, 228 (no. 5114).

9.   Clement VII was pope during the flood of 1530. For his papacy, see Maurizio Gattoni da Camogli, *Clemente VII e la geopolitica dello Stato Pontificio (1523–1534)* (Vatican City: Archivio Segreto Vaticano, 2002); Kenneth Gouwens and Sheryl E. Reiss, ed., *The Pontificate of Clement VII: History, Politics, Culture* (Aldershot: Ashgate, 2005); and Adriano Prosperi, "Clemente VII, papa," DBI 26 (1982): 237–59. None of these works treats the flood, however.

willingly and with the greatest pleasure to publish for the common enjoyment and benefit of all people of letters. Furthermore, I believe that many should read this little book. For, in addition to the excellent learning and knowledge that readers may acquire from it, it describes very clearly and lucidly the great floods of the Tiber and how much evil they have usually foreshadowed. As a result, diligent readers of these commentaries shall easily understand that innumerable, severe disasters threaten all Christians because of their very corrupt way of life, and they shall take care to adopt a truly Christian life to save themselves. Therefore, I again give you infinite thanks, most splendid lord, because we have been deeply moved by this saving benefit and because, with this agreement, you took thought for the immortality of this author's blossoming glory. Farewell. I beg you again and again that you count me among your clients.

[A4r] By the most severe edict of Clement VII, Pontifex Maximus, it is decreed that for the next five years no one but Francesco Minizio Calvo may print these commentaries or sell those that others may perhaps have dared to print.[10]

[A4v] An Epigram for the Most Holy Clement VII, Pontifex Maximus, by F. Maria Molza[11]
> *O Clement, do not despair that the Tiber made rivers of swollen waters equal to the sea*
> *And, threatening, flooded the besieged City.*

---

10. This is a privilege given by Clement VII to Calvo that gave him a monopoly on publishing Gómez's tract for five years. For a history of this early form of copyright, which is significantly different from the modern practice, see Christopher L.C.E. Witcombe, *Copyright in the Renaissance: Prints and the* Privilegio *in Sixteenth-Century Venice and Rome* (Leiden: Brill, 2004), xxix–xxxiii, 45–52, and 129–53. Papal granting of privileges for book publication in Rome was a development from the early sixteenth century.

11. Francesco Maria Molza (1489–1544), a poet from Modena. See Peter Hainsworth and David Robey, ed., *Oxford Companion to Italian Literature* (Oxford: Oxford University Press, 2002), 387–88; and Franco Pignatti, "Una poetica inondazione: Francesco Maria Molza sull'alluvione di Roma del 7–8 Ottobre 1530 (e in morte di Clemente VII)," *Roma nel Rinascimento* (2017): 391–404.

The floodwaters, now reduced to sky-blue puddles,
Offer you glad tidings.
For in this same way, your former kingdoms shall not contain you
but your great Empire shall equal
the ends of the Ocean.

≈

[Br] *On the origin, name, and divinity of the Tiber and on its floods*
and their effects by Luis Gómez, Auditor of Cases of the Holy Apostolic
Palace and Regent of the Holy Penitentiary

SECTION 1: THE ORIGIN, NAME, AND DIVINITY OF THE TIBER

It is quite clear that the Tiber River, as it flows down from its source in the Apennines, had multiple names among the ancients. However, there was a great dispute about the jurisdiction to which it belonged. For the Etruscans used to say that the Tiber was theirs, because it originated in Samnium, and they denied it had a Latin origin. Because it was the border of the Volturrenum Empire, as Fabius Pictor says, they called it Volturnus.[12] But because the town

---

12. Gómez was likely referring here to the pseudonymous works of Q. Fabius Pictor published by Giovanni Nanni, also known as Annius of Viterbo, O.P., in *Berosus Babilonicus De his quae praecesserunt inundationem terrarum. Item, Myrsilus de origine Tyrrhenorum. Cato in fragmentis. Archilocus in Epitheto de temporibus. Metasthenes de iudicio temporum. Philo in breviario temporum. Xenophon de equiuocis temporum. Sempronius de divisione Italiae. Q. Fab. Pictor de aureo saeculo & origine [sic] urbis Rhomae. Fragmentum Itinerarii Antonini Pii. Altercatio Adriani Augusti & Epictici. Cornelii Taciti de origine & situ Germanorum opusculum. C.C. de situ & moribus Germanorum* (Paris: n.p., 1511), fol. XXXv. On Annius as historian and forger, see Christopher R. Ligota, "Annius of Viterbo and His Historical Method," *Journal of the Warburg and Courtauld Institutes* 50 (1987): 44–57; Anthony Grafton, "Invention of Traditions and Traditions of Invention in Renaissance Europe: The Strange Case of Annius of Viterbo," in *The Transmission of Culture in Early Modern Europe,* Anthony Grafton and Ann Blair, ed. (Philadelphia: University of Pennsylvania Press, 1990), 8–38; and Walter Stephens, "When Pope Noah Ruled the Etruscans: Annius of Viterbo and His Forged 'Antiquities,'" *Studia Humanitatis: Essays in Honor of Salvatore Camporeale,* MLN Italian Issue Supplement 119 (2004): S201–23.

of Samnium, [which was] next to the sea and the Tiber, was a Roman colony, Rome claimed it as its own and called it Volturnus. Indeed, the error arose because the name of Volturnus belonged to both peoples for different reasons. For Volturnus was the god of the Tiber, as Varro reports in book 1 of the *De lingua latina*,[13] and the Etruscans claimed that he had [taken] his name and origin from them. Or [that it derived] from the royal city of Volturnum, which Pliny records in book 3;[14] or from Volturnum,[15] which used to be called Capua, which had been under the jurisdiction of the Etruscans, as can be seen in Livy book 4 of the *Ab Urbe condita*[16] and in Fabius Pictor *De origine Urbis*;[17] or from the Volturnus River, which, according to the testimony of Ptolemy and Pliny,[18] originates in Samnium, runs near Capua, and then flows into the sea; or from Vertumnus, who was a prince and god of the towns of Etruria and was worshiped in Rome as Janus, as Propertius testifies in book 4 of the *Elegies*[19] and as Donatus explains based on Horace's words in book 1 of the *Epistles*.[20]

By the divine will of Vertumnus it happened that Rome, which was swampy and not suitable for settlement due to the Tiber's floods, became comfortable and convenient. Indeed, after they performed sacrifices to Vertumnus, the Tiber went back to its riverbed, as

---

13. Var. *L.* 5.29.

14. Plin. *Nat.* 3.5.61.

15. Volturnum, which was an Etruscan fortified place between Casilinum and Capua, is now called Castel Volturno.

16. Liv. 4. 36.

17. Pseudo-Q. Fabius Pictor, *De aureo saeculo*, in Annius of Viterbo, ed., *Berosus Babilonicus De his quae praecesserunt inundationem terrarum*, fol. XXIX.

18. Ptol. *Geog.* 3.1; Plin. *Nat.* 3.5.61.

19. Prop. 4.2.

20. Here Gómez seems to refer mistakingly to two different comments relating to Volturnus. The comment on Horace was written by Porphyrius, not by Donatus (Porph. *Ad Hor. Ep.* 1.20). Donatus referred to Volturnus in a comment to Terentius (Don. *Ter. Ad.* 728). On this issue, see Maurizio Bettini, "Vertumnus: A God with no Identity," *I Quaderni del Ramo d'Oro On Line* 3 (2010): 320–34.

Fabius Pictor reports in book 1 of the *De aureo saeculo*. Therefore, amidst so great a dispute about antiquities, those who wished to remove any uncertainty about the Etruscan [origin of the] name, called the Tiber Tuscus, who was also a god of the Tuscans, as Propertius records in the elegy [dedicated] to Vertumnus.[21] But then, as years passed, the ancients' name Volturnus fell into disuse, and the river received many other names, [Bv] the sequence and propriety of which Annius explains at length in book 7,[22] as does Boccaccio in *De fluminibus*.[23] The main ones were these three: Tybris, Albula, and Tiber, as Tortelli deduces from Pliny[24] and [Virgil] Maro.[25] Nevertheless, in such disputes among the ancients, that [river] alone gained so much praise and glory that among the rivers of the world it became very famous everywhere in the songs of the poets. For it is superior to the Xanthus and to the Simoeis, renowned in the memory of the Greeks, according to Boccaccio book 7 of the *Genealogy*, not only for the issue of its prodigies but also, according to the passage of Ovid, *Metamorphosis* 2, for a certain force and power of the waters:

---

21. Prop. 4.2.

22. Pseudo-Q. Fabius Pictor, *De aureo saeculo*, fol. XXIXv.

23. Giovanni Boccaccio, *De montibus [et] sylvis, de fontibus, lacubus [et] fluminibus ac etiam de stagnis [et] paludibus, necnon [et] de maribus, seu diversis maris nominibus* s.v. Tyberis, in *Genealogiae Joannis Boccatii cum demonstrationibus in formis arborum designatis eiusdem de montibus [et] sylvis, de fontibus, lacubus [et] fluminibus ac etiam de stagnis [et] paludibus, necnon [et] de maribus, seu diversis maris nominibus* (Venice: Agostino Zani, 1511), fols. 155v–156r.

24. In his work on orthography, Giovanni Tortelli offers a discussion of the names for the Tiber in which a number of classical authors are cited. Virgil appears, as do Servius, Juvenal, Ovid, and Livy, but not Pliny. Pliny does, however, appear elsewhere in other discussions of similar names (e.g., "Tibur") and in Tortelli's work as a whole: *Ioannis Tortelii Aretini orthographia. Ioannis Tortelii Lima quædam per Georgium Vallam tractatum de orthographia* (Venice: Tacuino, 1495). For Tortelli, see Peter Fane-Saunders, *Pliny the Elder and the Emergence of Renaissance Architecture* (New York: Cambridge University Press, 2016), 51–54.

25. Verg. A. 8.330–32.

And the Tiber to whom the domination of the world was promised;[26]
and *Fasti,* book 4:

And you, Tiber, future father of powerful waters.[27]

The river, small and weak in the place where it first arises, then grows almost fifty times larger and becomes so great that, according to Pliny's testimony, it is navigable for any large ship and is a most calm trader of goods arriving from everywhere in the world.[28] Its riverbed was found to be so deep that when that famous obelisk of C. [Julius] Caesar (which today is seen at the Vatican) was to be brought through the mouth [*ostia*] of the Tiber,[29] they took the measure of its waters and found that there was as much water in it as in the Nile, as Pliny says in book 36.[30] It was said to be sacred due to the purity of its

26.   Giovanni Boccaccio, *The Genealogy of the Pagan Gods* 7.51, John Solomon, ed. and trans., 2 vols. (Cambridge, MA: Harvard University Press, 2011-17), 2:45; Ov. *Met.* 2.259. The Xanthus was a river in ancient Lycia (southwest Turkey). The Simoeis was a river on the Trojan Plain.

27.   Ov. *Fast.* 4.572.

28.   Plin. *Nat.* 3.5.53. Gómez here personifies the Tiber, making it the "one who trades" goods from around the world.

29.   Gómez plays here with the word *ostia*, which means both "mouths" of a river and the name of Rome's port, Ostia.

30.   Plin. *Nat.* 36.14.70. Gómez refers to the Vatican obelisk, which had been transported from Egypt in 41 CE by Emperor Caligula. It had been carried by ship to the harbor at Ostia and then transported up the Tiber to Caligula's circus in the Ager Vaticanus. In the intervening centuries, without being moved, St. Peter's Basilica rose next to the ancient monument, so that in 1531 it was standing in an obscure corner near the Old Sacristy of the basilica. In 1586 it would be moved with much acclaim to the center of St. Peter's Square, where it stands today. See Géza Alföldy, *Der Obelisk auf dem Petersplatz in Rom: Ein historische Monument der Antike* (Heidelberg: Carl Winter, 1990); Ferdinando Castagnoli, *Il Vaticano nell'antichità classica* (Vatican City: Biblioteca Apostolica Vaticana, 1992); Brian A. Curran, Anthony Grafton, Pamela O. Long, and Benjamin Weiss, *Obelisk: A History* (Cambridge, MA: Burndy Library and MIT Press, 2009), esp. 102–39; Bern Dibner, *Moving the Obelisks* (1950; repr. Norwalk, CT: Burndy Library, 1991), 20–43; Cesare D'Onofrio, *Gli obelischi di Roma: Storia e urbanistica di una città dall'età antica al XX secolo,* 3rd ed. (Rome: Romana Società

uncorrupted waters, so that it was believed to possess divinity. Even though Aeneas Silvius in *Epistle* 103 mocks the esteem for its divinity because of [the river's] multiple origins, nevertheless, it is certain that the ancients, out of respect for its divinity, did not want to build on its banks. With regard to the divinity of the Tiber, they also report that a certain vestal virgin drew water from the Tiber with a sieve and it did not drain away.[31] Likewise, [they tell] that the virgin Cloelia, one of the hostages given to Porsena, deceived the guards, lead a column of virgins, and swam across the Tiber unharmed among the spears and arrows of the enemies, according to Livy, book 2.[32] Juvenal writes on this in *Satire* 6:

> The virgin who swam across the Tiber, boundary of the empire.[33]

These authors also ascribe to the divinity [of the Tiber] what they attest about Horatius Cocles, who, after cutting the Pons Sublicius,[34] said:

> O Father Tiberinus, I solemnly pray that you accept these arms and this soldier [by making] the river favorable.[35]

Editrice, 1992), 143–84; Erik Iversen, *Obelisks in Exile* 1: *The Obelisks of Rome* (Copenhagen: GEC Gad, 1968), 19–46; Paolo Liverani, *La topografia antica del Vaticano* (Vatican City: Monumenti, Musei e Gallerie Pontificie, 1999), 21–28 for the circus; Paolo Carafa and Paola Pacchiarotti, "Region XIV Transtiberim," in *Atlas of Ancient Rome: Biography and Portraits of the City*, 2 vols., Andrea Carandini and Paolo Carafa, ed.; Andrew Campbell Halavais, trans. (Princeton, NJ: Princeton University Press, 2017), 1:549–82, at 558.

31. According to the myth, the vestal virgin Tuccia was falsely accused of having broken her vow of chastity or, according to a different version, of having let the sacred fire be extinguished. She proved her innocence by carrying the water of the Tiber to the temple of Vesta in a sieve. See Robert E. Bell, *Women of Classical Mythology: A Biographical Dictionary* (Oxford: Oxford University Press, 1993), 427.

32. Liv. 2.13.6.

33. In the modern edition, Juv. 8.265.

34. See p 43 n. 85.

35. Liv. 2.10.11. According to most ancient sources, Horatius Cocles was a legendary hero who single-handedly defended the right bank of the Tiber

No one would easily doubt that what happened to the virgin Cloelia, a very inexperienced swimmer, should be attributed to the hidden divinity of the Tiber, if one notes that Horatius Cocles was an expert swimmer. For the Pamphylian Sea parted and offered a dry path to Alexander the Great and his soldiers who were invading the Persian Empire [B2r], and the Red Sea once provided the same thing to Moses. (Josephus is the authority for both in the last chapter of book 2 of the *Jewish Antiquities*.)[36] Why then should we not suppose that this same thing could happen with the Tiber? And who would think that what happened to Alexander, [who was] otherwise a tyrant, did not happen to Horatius Cocles, defender of the fatherland? Indeed, who would not ascribe to a certain hidden divinity of the Tiber that its shallows kept Romulus and Remus safe on its banks, and that an island was created by its overflowing waters?[37] But human nature has never been more resistant than when it is asked to believe in miracles. Be that as it may, we have gathered another sign of divinity from something else: that the Tiber's waters, especially those within the city walls, remain uncorrupted everywhere, so that, even when carried to distant lands, they keep the same good taste that they usually have in Rome.[38] In truth, we have not discovered whether this happens by virtue of a certain religious

---

from the Etruscans. He gave the Romans time to cut the bridge to prevent the invasion and then saved himself by swimming to the other side of the river.

36. See Joseph. *A.J.* 2.339 (Moses), 2.348 (Alexander the Great).

37. I.e., the Tiber Island.

38. There was a debate among physicians (manifest in printed tracts from the mid-sixteenth century) about whether Tiber water was healthy to drink or not. One physician, Giovanni Battista Modio, *Il Tevere* (Rome: Vincenzo Luchino, 1556), fols. 8v–8r, argued against the salubrity of the river water and railed against the physicians who had encouraged Pope Clement VII to carry Tiber water with him on trips outside of Rome. Such papal portage of Tiber water was apparently the rule at this time, since one of the proponents of the goodness of Tiber water, Alessandro Traiano Petroni, noted that Pope Paul III (r.1534–49) always carried it when traveling outside the city. See Petroni, *De victu romanorum et de sanitate tuenda libri quinque* (Rome: Stamperia del Popolo Romano, 1581), 37. In the passage above, Gómez is probably referring to Clement VII's portage of Tiber water. See Andretta, "Les médecins du Tibre"; Bonaccorso, "Roma e le sue acque potabili"; and Long, *Engineering the Eternal City*, 23–24.

disposition of a city consecrated with the blood of so many martyrs, by some hidden power of nature, or because the Tiber is not enmeshed in swamps and pools. We may also wish to mention another reason: that the water of the Tiber, even when very filtered, wherever it may be, always retains sand or silt as a matrix in a hidden and subtle natural combination, so that it is preserved uncorrupted longer and everywhere. We have learned from a convincing experiment that waters not mixed with sand easily putrefy; or rather, their nature has been corrupted by a lack of sand. If they are mixed with sand, they are easily preserved. Indeed, Procopius in book 3 of the *Persian War* reports that when Antonia, wife of Belisarius, discovered that all the water that runs near Etna is easily corrupted, she ordered that glass vessels be filled, placed in the hold of the ship where the sun barely penetrated, and that they be covered in sand, surrounding the place on all sides with fencing.[39] Through this experiment, it turned out that the water remained uncorrupted and provided sailors a drink of sweet water. For we already know from experience that wine and oil keep longer in dregs and residue and deteriorate immediately when these are not present.

We must suppose that the ancients gave sacred honor to the water of the Tiber for this reason. For they thought it was important both to religion and divinity if, before they embarked on religious rites, they bathed in the water of the Tiber three times in the morning and purified themselves, as Juvenal reports in *Satire* 6, when he says:

> In the morning, she will bathe in the Tiber three times, and in these
> Eddies she will wash clean her timid head;[40]

and Persius in *Satire* 2:

> So that you may sanctify these prayers, in the Tiber River
> Dip your head twice and three times in the morning and with the
> river purge the night.[41]

39. Procop. *Vand.* 1.13.24. Gómez correctly reports the story but misplaces it within Procopius' corpus.

40. Juv. 6.523–24. In this satire against women, Juvenal mentions these ablutions in the Tiber among other rituals that Roman matrons performed and criticizes them for being superstitious.

41. Pers. 2.15–16. Persius explains that ablutions in the Tiber are the only remedy against impurity that comes from dishonest prayers. Here the night is mentioned as another source of impurity, generated by sleep, dreams, and sex.

[B2v] Apuleius also records this. Relevant here is this passage from book 2 of Horace's *Sermones*:

> *If the cold quartan [fever] leaves my boy,*
> *On the morning when you impose fasting,*
> *He will stand naked in the Tiber. Luck or the physician*
> *May save the sick [boy], but thoughtlessly the raving mother will*
>   *kill him*
>
> *By immersing him in ice-cold water and bringing back his fever.*[42]

Yet, alongside these natural gifts, the river is otherwise ferocious and like a tyrant. It sometimes snatches swimmers and swallows even the most experienced in its frightening whirlpools. Its floods, although they were always harmful, were also considered by the ancients to be portents. To be sure, Pliny in book 3 of the *Natural History* had a different view, claiming that the Tiber was, in truth, more sacred than savage when it rose suddenly — but he had little experience of its savagery.[43] For among the twenty-three epithets that Joannes Ravisius Textor[44] gathered from various texts, ancients called the Tiber "Rapidus" or "Rumon," as if its floodwaters chewed upon and devoured its banks, as Servius in his commentary to *Aeneid* 8 testifies. There he adds that in religious rites it was called

---

42. Hor. *S.* 2.3.290–94. *Sermones* is another name for the *Satires*. Gómez cites this passage concerning a mother who prays to Jupiter to cure her sick boy, promising that if he does, she will have the boy stand naked in the Tiber. Here Horace is making fun of superstitious people who fear the gods.

43. Plin. *Nat.* 3.5.55.

44. Joannes Ravisius Textor, *Specimen epithetorum* (Paris: n.p., 1518), 281. Joannes Ravisius Textor (1493–1522) was a French humanist whose writings included a manual of epithets for university students. See Nathaël Istasse, "Joannes Ravisius Textor: Mise au point biographique," *Bibliothèque d'Humanisme et Renaissance* 69 (2007): 691–703; idem, "Le *Specimen Epithetorum* (1518) et le *Epitheta* (1524): J. Ravisius Textor compilateur et créateur," in *L'épithète, la rime et la raison: La lexicographie poétique en Europe, XVIe–XVIIe siècles*, S. Hache and A.-P. Pouey-Mounou, ed. (Paris: Classiques Garniers, 2015), 79–121; and I.D. McFarlane, "Reflections on Ravisius Textor's *Specimen Epithetorum*," in *Classical Influences on European Culture, A.D. 1500–1700*, R.R. Bolgar, ed. (Cambridge: Cambridge University Press, 2010), 81–90.

"Serra" [i.e., saw].[45] This is why Virgil, when speaking about the Tiber in that same passage, [says]:

> And cutting up fertile fields;[46]

and Ovid book 1 of the *Fasti*:

> The wave of the sandy Tiber shaves the [river's] sides.[47]

We have learned this most bitter lesson both from the examples provided by the ancients and especially from the wretched flood of our times, which we will describe in its own place. But now that we have come to mentioning the Tiber's floods, it will be worthwhile to investigate carefully whether those ancient floods that Livy and other ancient authors record are greater than the more recent ones that are said to have happened after the birth of Christ. Certainly, this issue is ambiguous, obscure, full of conjecture, and varies according to one's point of view. Since there are many opinions, and they are in conflict, those that are judged to be stronger and more demonstrable will shine a brighter light on this matter for us.

Here we offer conjectures that might persuade us that ancient floods were greater.[48] The first is that it is well known that long ago the area between the Palatine and the Capitoline[49] [Fig. 3] was not very suitable for habitation due to the flooding of the Tiber. For this reason, that place was marshy and produced unhealthy air, as Fabius

---

45. Serv. *A.* 8.63.

46. Verg. *A.* 8.63.

47. Ov. *Fast.* 1.24.

48. The question that Gómez asks, whether ancient floods or floods in his own time were worse, cannot be resolved precisely because the exact heights of ancient and early medieval floods are unknown before the first Roman flood marker of February 2, 1230. It is clear nevertheless that severe floods occurred in ancient Rome. As Aldrete has convincingly argued, most elite Romans in the ancient city lived on the hills, and although they carefully protected grain supplies by building flood-proof grain warehouses and occasionally undertook anti-flooding measures on the river, they did not actually care very much about what happened to the plebs who, for the most part, lived on the floodplain. See Aldrete, *Floods,* 51–90, 225–31.

49. I.e., the valley of the Roman Forum.

Fig. 3. Roman Forum viewed from the Palatine. Drawing by Maarten van Heemskerck, Berlin, Berliner Kupferstichkabinett, 79d2a12r.

Pictor testifies in book 1 of the *On the Golden Age*.[50] Therefore, given the fact that the water reached this place, it is easy to understand that those ancient floods were greater than the more recent ones. An obvious line of reasoning proves this. For it is clear that, if the Tiber's waters at that time [B3r] were even more abundant and copious, we must wonder why, when heavy rains came, they did not also inundate the hills themselves. For we read that Claudius Caesar at great expense led many streams, springs, and lakes to the Tiber. In addition to the water intended for waste management, nineteen aqueducts also flowed into it, as Sextus Rufus testifies.[51] Later, Theodoric, king of the

---

50. Pseudo-Q. Fabius Pictor, *De aureo saeculo*, fol. XXIXv.

51. Gómez here refers to a collection of texts known now as the Regionary Catalogs. They have come down to us in two versions, the "Curiosum urbis Romae Regionum XIIII" and the "Notitia urbis Romae," both of which list nineteen aqueducts. See Arvast Nordh, *Libellus de regionibus urbis Romae* (Lund: C.W.K. Gleerup, 1949), 101–2; and Roberto Valentini and Giuseppe Zucchetti, ed., *Codice topografico della città di Roma*, 4 vols. (Rome: Tipografia del Senato, 1940–53), 1:154–55 (*Curiosum*), and 1:191–92 (*Notitia*). Gómez refers to one Sextus Rufus, to whom the work entitled *De regionibus urbis Romae* was attributed. Scholars no longer think that Sextus Rufus was a real person. These texts were created in the

Fig. 4. Remains of the Aqueduct of Nero. From Giovanni Battista Piranesi, Vedute di Roma. *Etching, 1754.*

Ostrogoths, reclaimed these aqueducts, which were falling into ruin, from the damage inflicted by their old age [Fig. 4].

---

fourth century CE and listed buildings and other features in each of the fourteen Augustan *regiones* or districts of Rome. Centuries later, during the fifteenth century, students of ancient Roman topography used them while investigating Roman ruins and made many additions. On the regionary catalogs, see Javier Arce, "El inventario di Roma: *Curiosum y Notitia,*" in *The Transformations of* Urbs Roma *in Late Antiquity,* W.V. Harris, ed., *Journal of Roman Archaeology,* Supplementary Series 33 (1999): 15–22; André Chastagnol, "Les régionnaires de Rome," in *Les littératures techniques dans l'antiquité romaine: Statut, public et destination, tradition,* Claude Nicolet, ed. (Geneva: Foundation Hardt, 1996), 179–97; Simon Alistair Hosie, "'Cataloguing the Empire': The Regionary Catalogues and the Role and Purpose of Bureaucratic Inventories" (MPhil diss.: University of Sheffield, 2016); and Domenico Palombi, "Regiones Quattuordecim (Topographia)," LTUR 4:199–204. For the later (fifteenth-century) uses of these catalogs, see Philip Jacks, *The Antiquarian and the Myth of Antiquity: The Origins of Rome in Renaissance Thought* (Cambridge: Cambridge University Press, 1993), 93–95, 115–16, 157–61; and Frances Muecke, "Humanists in the Roman Forum," *Papers of the British School at Rome* 71 (2003): 207–33.

Fourteen of these still flowed at the time of Pope Silverius until the barbarians under the command of Vitiges cut them off.[52] Pope Hadrian I restored some of them at great expense, as Damasus and Platina testify.[53] Indeed, the great combined mass of these waters flowed down into the Tiber. Those seven swift streams, which Marcus Agrippa had ordered to be led into the underground drains as powerful torrents to wash everything away, were also directed into [the Tiber], as Strabo and Cassiodorus in book 4 of his *Letters* record.[54] As a consequence, Pliny in book 36 says that the entire city was supported on arches and navigable underneath in such a way that if someone carefully considered the abundance of water that

52. Procop. *Goth.* 1.19.

53. Bartolomeo Platina, *Platynae historici Liber de vita Christi ac omnium pontificum aa. 1–1474,* Giacinto Gaida, ed., RIS 3.1 (Città di Castello: Scipione Lapi, 1913–1932), 137 s.n. Hadrianus I. "Damasus" here refers to the *Liber Pontificalis,* the early sections of which were sometimes attributed to Pope Damasus I. For Hadrian I, see Louis Duchesne, ed., *Liber Pontificalis,* 2 vols. (Paris: Ernst Thorin, 1886), 1:504–5, c.97: Hadrianus.

54. The reference here is uncertain. There is no reference to the Tiber in Cassiodorus, *Variae* 4, but the Roman sewers are praised in *Variae* 3.30.2 (King Theodoric to Arcolicus, City Prefect), Theodor Mommsen, ed., MGH, *Auctores Antiquissimi* 12 (Berlin: Weidman, 1894), 94–95; or *Variae* 10.12.2 (King Theoderic to the Roman Senate), 305. The seven swift streams (*septem rapidissimi amnes*) that flow like torrents could refer to the seven aqueducts that existed in Rome at the time of Agrippa during the reign of Augustus (Acqua Appia, Anio Vetus, Acqua Marcia, Acqua Tepula, Acqua Giulia, Acqua Vergine, and Acqua Alsietina). Strabo uses similar terms when he describes the underground channels and sewers to which Agrippa had dedicated much attention. Strabo says that they were so large that wagons loaded with hay could pass through them and adds that the supply of water from the aqueducts was so abundant that it flowed through the underground channels just like in rivers (Str. 5.3.8). For a study of some of the aqueducts and other water issues in the ancient city, see Peter J. Aicher, *Guide to the Aqueducts of Ancient Rome* (Wauconda, IL: Bolchazy-Carducci, 1995); Rabun Taylor, *Public Needs and Private Pleasures: Water Distribution, the Tiber River, and the Urban Development of Ancient Rome* (Rome: L'"Erma" di Bretschneider, 2000); and Marcello Turci, "The Aqueducts," in *Atlas of Ancient Rome,* Carandini and Carafa, 1:92–100.

was publicly available for baths, pools, houses, channels, gardens, suburban villas, and then considered the arches constructed, the hills pierced, and the valleys leveled, he would say that there was nothing more wondrous in the whole world.[55]

We ought therefore to suppose that with such a superabundance of water the Tiber long ago was more swollen, full, and deep than now because of the quantity of water, so that it flooded more easily and more extensively. A narrowing of its banks added to this, for in such a full and populous city they did not think it fitting that such an abundance of water flow around freely. Consequently, Marcus Agrippa made its riverbed narrower. Emperor Aurelian constrained the Tiber within its banks with brick walls on both sides all the way to the sea, the remains of which still exist. Therefore, who would be surprised if the waters from downpours burst into great and astonishing floods when they reach such a full and swollen river confined within its banks? We therefore now believe what Pliny said to have been true: that at that time the Tiber contained as much water as the Nile.[56] For this reason, we read that the Senate often discussed how to control the floods and restrain that great force of water. About this issue, it is believed that Cicero defended a case in front of the consuls and ten ambassadors.[57] Likewise, there was an old dispute, which was never pursued with greater intensity than in the time of Emperor Tiberius. For, as Cornelius Tacitus notes in his first book:

> In that year the Tiber, swollen by continuous rain, caused great damage to people and buildings and burst forth with great violence. [B3v] Because it had so worried all the Romans, Asinius Gallus thought that they must consult the Sibylline Books, unless Tiberius forbade it. They therefore appointed two men, Atteius Capito and Quintus Aruntius, to control the force of the river and to make sure that the streams and lakes by which it was increased were diverted. Then, the delegations of the municipal towns and colonies were heard in

---

55. Plin. *Nat.* 36.24.123.

56. See p. 25 n. 30.

57. In 54 BCE, Cicero represented the city of Rieti against the city of Terni in a dispute discussed in front of the Roman Senate about the flooding of Terni caused by the river Nera (Cic. *Att.* 4.15.5).

the Senate, with the Florentines begging that the Chiana River not be moved from its usual riverbed and diverted into the Arno River, for this would damage them. Agreeing with them, the people of Interamna argued that the very fertile fields of Italy would go to ruin if the Nera River, reduced to rivulets, was turned into a marsh (for this was the plan). Nor were the people of Rieti silent: they refused to block Lake Velino, which flowed into the Nera, because it would have poured out into the surrounding area. They argued that nature took very good care of human affairs by providing rivers with their own outlets and their own courses, sources, and banks. They also said that it was necessary to respect the religions of allies who dedicated rites, groves, and altars to the fatherly rivers, and they did not want the Tiber, utterly deprived of its tributaries, to flow with less glory. Whether it was the requests of the colonies, or the difficulties of the project, or religious awe that prevailed, the Senate approved the opinion of Piso, who had proposed that nothing should be changed.[58]

From these words of Tacitus, it is quite clear how much trouble the floods of the Tiber had given to the Roman people, even if most of them lived on the hills. Therefore, we may be permitted to suppose that in those times the floods were greater and higher than the ones that have happened in our times. Indeed, we must believe that Trajan wanted to extend to the sea that huge channel[59] that had already been started by another emperor,[60] so that the swollen waters of the Tiber would have an outlet, just as Darius and the Ptolemaic kings did with the Nile, as Diodorus attests.[61] We believe that Julius Caesar was moved to drain the Fucine Lake and to make a road from the Adriatic

---

58. Tac. *Ann.* 1.76; 1.79.

59. The *Fossa Traiana* (now Fiumicino Canal) is an artificial channel that Emperor Trajan built as part of a renewed port north of Ostia, which enlarged the earlier port of Claudius. The channel linked the Tiber to the sea and, along with other minor channels, was meant to prevent flooding caused by the river. For the *Fossa Traiana*, see Federico Ugolini, *Visualizing Harbours in the Classical World: Iconography and Representation around the Mediterranean* (London: Bloomsbury, 2020), 21.

60. I.e., Claudius.

61. Diod. Sic. 1.33.

Sea through the ridge of the Apennines up to the Tiber for no other purpose than to make the floods less intense and easier to endure.[62] These are the arguments that seem to support this thesis.

But the contrary argument that the floods of our time exceed those of ancient times goes like this. The exacting maintenance to keep the Tiber clear failed along with the empire. For, just as all those admirable embankments were abandoned, so the riverbed of the Tiber also started to be neglected. To tell the truth, [such was the neglect] that in our own time, the via Giulia and the buildings constructed most recently on both banks occupy a good portion of its former bed.[63] What is left of this narrow riverbed is filled with the ruins of bridges and buildings and with the refuse of the entire city and packed with fragments of stones and with sand. We must therefore wonder why, with its watercourse so impeded, it does not flood more often, [B4r] given that formerly, even when its riverbed was wider and very well maintained, it flooded very frequently. You would weep if you now saw the Tiber, which the ancients called smooth because its riverbed was clean, without obstacles, and freely flowing. For the Senate and Augustus had appointed some curators for this matter, as some inscriptions show that were excavated not long ago near the bridge to the Vatican.[64] Indeed, as Suetonius Tranquillus reports,

> Rome has been previously subject to floods, and to control them Augustus enlarged the Tiber's riverbed and cleaned it, since it had been filled over time by debris and collapsed buildings.[65]

But today, since that maintenance has ceased, we should instead call the Tiber slow or sluggish or difficult. For this reason, it swells easily, as happened in the time of Aurelian, when it was swollen and

---

62. For a study of the draining of Lake Fucino, see Philippe Leveau, "Mentalité économique et grands travaux: Le drainage du Lac Fucin aux origines d'un modèle," *Annales ESC* 48 (1993): 3–36.

63. For the via Giulia, built by Pope Julius II in 1508, see pp. 66–67 n. 151.

64. I.e., Ponte Sant'Angelo. For the office of the curators of the Tiber, see Anna Lonardi, *La* cura riparum et alvei Tiberis: *Storiografia, prosopografia e fonti epigrafiche*, BAR International Series no. 2464 (Oxford: BAR Publishing, 2013).

65. Suet. *Aug.* 30.

slow because of the rubble and ruins of the city. This magnanimous prince therefore improved the speed of the swollen riverbed by dredging the Tiber's bottom, as Flavius Vopiscus attests.[66] Cyrus, king of the Persians, also did this with the Indus. For, because it was slowed by the abundance of water and therefore subject to floods, he divided its course by digging multiple channels. Herodotus says that their number was 460 and that it was reduced to such a small size that it was possible to cross it with dry feet.[67] We read that Osiris did the same thing with the Nile, which often used to flood, as Diodorus says.[68] King Myris also dug a lake near Memphis above the city, which had a circumference of 360 stadia and was 50 cubits deep.[69] When the Nile surged, the lake received these waters and defeated the river's increase. In the same way, at the Fucine Lake, Claudius tunneled through the mountain and channeled the excess water into the river; and we must suppose that the same thing was done to Lake Velino by M[anius] Curio [Dentatus] for the same reason. Caesar had also decided to create as many channels as possible in Lleida to divert some part of the Segre. Near the Euphrates he added several lakes as well as embankments to reduce the force of the river, so that it would not destroy the houses of the city. For this reason, Tarquinius Priscus straightened the Tiber's riverbed. Then, because the Tiber was still winding, the aedile Marcus Agrippa made it straighter, altered the riverbed, and reinforced it by placing massive stone embankments along both banks. For, as Servius in his commentary to *Aeneid* 8 and Pomponio [Leto] say, the Tiber beneath the Capitoline had a bend that reached the foot of the Palatine at the ficus Ruminalis, where

---

66.   SHA, *Aurel.* 47. Flavius Vopiscus, who is considered to be one of the authors of the *Historia Augusta*, reports that Emperor Aurelian built up the banks of the Tiber and dredged the shallows of the riverbed.

67.   Hdt. 1.189–91. The number of channels reported in the modern edition of Herodotus is 360.

68.   Diod. Sic. 1.19.5.

69.   Diod. Sic. 1.52.1. A *stadium* = 625 *pedes*, while one *pes* = c.1 ft/30.5 cm. A *cubitum* = c.18″/46 cm. Gómez's dimensions of 360 *stadia* in circumference and 50 cubits deep equals about 42.5 miles/71 km in circumference and 75 ft/23m deep.

Romulus and Remus came ashore.[70] Later, in the same place, there was the Circus between the Palatine and the Capitoline, where the Lupercal was, as Fabius Pictor relates in book 2.[71]

This is why the floods, which Vertumnus prevented when sacrifices were performed (according to Servius),[72] seemed destructive at that time but were not so troublesome to the city after the riverbed was altered, [B4v] though the city did still flood sometimes. But in our time, the new Rome has been built in low-lying areas next to the Tiber, the maintenance of the river has been completely abandoned, and its riverbed has been restricted and reduced by rubble and ruins to the smallest and narrowest of passages. It therefore produces frequent and more damaging floods, which we must believe are far greater than the ones in ancient times. An inscription excavated near the house of the Very Reverend Father Lord Tommaso da Prato,

---

70. Serv. A. 8.90. Giulio Pomponio Leto, *De romanae Urbis vetustate noviter impressus* (Rome: Giacomo Mazzocchi 1515), C2v. The *ficus Ruminalis* was a sacred fig tree, the name of which is linked to Rumina, ancient goddess of nursing, and is connected to the foundation myth of Rome. After they had been abandoned in a cradle, the twins Romulus and Remus, sons of Mars and Rhea Silvia, a vestal virgin of Alba Longa, came ashore here, carried by a Tiber flood. According to ancient sources, the tree grew in front of a cave called the Lupercal, a sanctuary dedicated to Faunus, a Latin silvan deity, at the southwest foot of the Palatine overlooking the Tiber and the valley of the Circus Maximus. For the debate about the topographical identification of the Lupercal, see Krešimir Vuković, "The Topography of the Lupercalia," *Papers of the British School at Rome* 86 (2018): 37–60.

71. It is not clear why Gómez described the location of the Circus Maximus as lying between the Palatine and the Capitoline, since the valley in which it lies is between the Palatine and the Aventine. A possible explanation could be that he had just described the marshy area at the foot of the Capitoline (and the Palatine) that was frequently affected by floods before the construction of the Cloaca Maxima in the sixth century BCE. This marsh extended south toward the Aventine and the valley of the Circus Maximus and can be described as a single large, low area. See Pseudo-Q. Fabius Pictor, *De aureo saeculo*, XXIXv–XXXr. For the valley of the Circus Maximus in antiquity, see Chiara Bariviera, "Region XI Circus Maximus," 421–25," in Carandini and Carafa, 1:421–25.

72. Serv. A. 8.90, 98.

who now deservedly holds the position of datary, makes clear that the ancient bed of the Tiber extended to this place.[73]

My kind reader will judge which of these opposing conjectures seem the more likely to persuade the opposite side. My own judgment on these matters I shall not dare to offer, since it is enough that I have laid out the conjectures with which we have rendered the matter uncertain. Given the most recent and very harsh flood of the Tiber, in which I suffered serious damage, I would not want to be considered an unreliable judge because I pronounced the ancient floods to be greater. I never saw these nor can understand them without conjecture, especially when we see before our very eyes the pain inflicted on mortals by this latest flood. It is therefore worth the effort in this second part to enumerate all those floods that happened in Rome through the ages, so that we may be consoled by the adversities of past times and bear more easily the present troubles as if we shared the same fate.

SECTION 2: THE PAST FLOODS OF THE TIBER

Amid this great series of events, it remains for us to narrate in chronological order all those floods recorded by ancient and more recent writers. The subject is certainly full of sorrow and pain, but it has much that is pleasing. For nature has made it so that human beings are fascinated more by reading about human adversity and calamity than about prosperity and success. We shall easily satisfy this fascination if we concisely narrate this subject, which seemed to need longer elaboration. We shall proceed in this way: we will describe only the extraordinary and remarkable floods and omit the small and less remarkable ones that did not trouble or amaze [Cr] the Roman people. We will describe only those caused by the Tiber. For we are not investigating the multiple rises of the sea nor the floods of all the rivers from which some provinces, such as Achaea,[74] took their name, even though many that we record were caused by the prodigious Nile, the Po, and the Danube, the most famous rivers

---

73. This inscription is quoted at the beginning of this treatise. See pp. 18–19 nn. 5 and 6.

74. A region of Greece in the northern Peloponnese. Here Gómez may be using an etymology of Achaea meaning "without land."

in the world. Rather, for so great a task, it will be enough for us to select only those floods that we judge relevant to our plan.

FLOODS OF THE TIBER BEFORE THE COMING OF CHRIST[75]

First flood [414 BCE]

In the memory of the ancients, the first flood that the Tiber caused was the one which, because of its magnitude, completely ended or at least delayed the war between the Veians and the Roman people. For, as Livy records in book 4 of *From the Founding of the City*:

> After overflowing its banks, the Tiber destroyed the fields with particularly severe damage to the country-estates. At the same time, their defeat suffered three years before prevented the Aequi from bringing help to the Bolae, who were a people of the same stock.[76]

From these words it is easy to conclude that this flood was of no small importance, given that it was able to recall the majesty of the leaders of the Roman people from their public affairs.

Second flood [215 BCE]

Of no lesser importance was the Tiber flood that the same Livy reports in book 3 of the *Second Punic War*. For he says that in the year in which Q. Fabius Maximus and Marcus Marcellus were consuls, there was a lot of rain and snow that caused the Tiber to flood the fields with great destruction of houses and the death of many animals and people.[77] From the words of Livy we can contemplate the wretched condition of those times when almost all of Italy burned with the blazing torches of wars. For at that moment the barbarian Hannibal, a glorious enemy, was pressing at the gates to extinguish the name of the Romans. Lest the city suffer from just one great evil, a flood of the Tiber, full of damage and with the most dreadful result, joined as his ally. But at last the virtue and constancy of the Roman people prevailed, admonishing posterity to endure dangers bravely.

---

75. Gómez refers here to the birth or *"adventus"* of Christ, which was the key moment in the *anno domini* (year of the Lord) dating system.

76. Liv. 4.49.3. See also Aldrete, *Floods*, 16.

77. Liv. 24.9.6. See also Aldrete, *Floods*, 17.

Third flood [202 BCE]
Here I would insert another flood, which the same Livy records in book 10 of the *Punic War*,[78] that inundated the Circus Flaminius, had I not seen that it was judged to be unimportant because [the circus] was intended [just] for the amusement of the Roman people. At that time, the games in honor of Apollo were staged outside Porta Collina, near the temple of Venus Erycina; and what would have caused mostly pain and grief, brought applause and pleasure.[79] [Cv] But at that time, Roman affairs were so favorable and prosperous that what would otherwise have been a lamentable prodigy was turned to the good with the aid of fortune.

Fourth flood [193 BCE]
An almost identical flood happened at the time of the consul Q. [Caecilius] Metellus, which was taken as a prodigy.[80] For fortune is fickle: it transforms the same thing depending on circumstances. For, if we believe Livy in book 5 on the *Macedonian War*, abundant waters in that year caused the Tiber to flood all the low-lying areas of the city and to pull down several buildings around Porta Flumentana.[81] Therefore,

78. Liv. 30.38.10–12. See also Aldrete, *Floods*, 17.

79. The Circus Flaminius was located in the southern area of the Campus Martius. See Alessandro Viscogliosi, "Circus Flaminius," LTUR 1:269–72. According to Livy, in 202 BCE the circus flooded (*circo inundato*), and for this reason the games were hosted instead in the area of the temple of Venus Erycina outside Porta Collina, the Servian gate from which the via Salaria and via Nomentana issued. While many scholars interpret the circus as being the Circus Flaminius, in the passage cited by Gómez Livy seems to refer to the Circus Maximus. Elsewhere, while speaking of the institution of the *ludi* (i.e., games) during the Punic War, Livy (25.12) stated that the *ludi Apollinares* were held in the Circus Maximus. If this is correct, the flood in 202 BCE might not have affected the area of the Circus Flaminius but rather that of the Circus Maximus.

80. Here Gómez refers to Caecilius Metellus as "consul," even though he did not hold the consulship in this year. He had been consul in 206 BCE.

81. Liv. 35.9.2–3. See also Aldrete, *Floods*, 17. The Porta Flumentana was a gate of the Servian walls situated between the Capitoline and the Aventine. Its name derives from its proximity to the Tiber (*flumen* = river). For a recent discussion about its location, see Timothy Peter Wiseman, "Walls,

if we can postulate future events from present ones, we must think that [that flood] brought great damage to the city. For the Tiber never overflowed without portending something remarkably bad.

Fifth flood [192 BCE]
But among all other water disasters, we are compelled to wonder most at the [flood] at the time of consul Cn. Domitius [Ahenobarbus]. It filled the bed of the Tiber and made it swell so much that, propelled by a more damaging current than the previous one, [the river] tore down bridges, destroyed many buildings, dragged away livestock in the fields, and brought devastation to country estates. Indeed, there was so much rain that a huge rock, displaced by the rain or by an earthquake too small to be felt otherwise, fell from the Capitoline into the Vicus Iugarius and killed many.[82] Livy reports this flood along with other great prodigies in the same book.[83]

Sixth flood [189 BCE]
The Tiber flood that — according to Livy's report in book 8 of the *Macedonian War* — affected the city twelve times in the year when Cn. Manlius [Vulso] was consul might seem more violent.[84] Yet, the one that we just mentioned was greater than all the others. For it brought so much damage, so much loss of life, and the destruction of so many buildings that, were it to be described in words, no greater flood could be imagined. Indeed, what force of water could have been as great as to destroy two bridges built upon massive piers? Perhaps one might say that the Pons Sublicius, which was one of the two bridges destroyed, was made of wood and therefore could be destroyed without effort. But this is false. Let us consider

Gates and Stories: Detecting Rome's Riverside Defenses," *Papers of the British School at Rome* 89 (2021): 9–40, at 19–22.

82. The street called Vicus Iugarius, wrapping around the foot of the Capitoline, led from the Forum to the Porta Carmentalis, between the Capitoline and the Palatine, along a path that partially corresponds to the modern via della Consolazione. See Paola Virgili, "Vicus Iugarius," LTUR 5:169–70.

83. Liv. 35.21.5–6.

84. 189 BCE. See Liv. 38.28.4 (the Tiber flooded twelve times); Livy 35.21 (the flood destroyed two bridges). See also Aldrete, *Floods*, 18.

the chronology. Ancus Marcius built the Pons Sublicius out of wood as the first of the bridges, as Livy and Pliny report when they offer an account of its construction. However, [this bridge was] already made out of stone at the time of this flood.[85] For the praetor Aemilius Lepidus, from whom it took its name, had made it out of stone, as Pomponio Leto, Fabrizio Varano, Albertino, Volterrano, and other recent [authors] report in their collectanea on the city.[86] Yet, Domizio Calderini, [Antonio] Mancinelli, and some new grammarians [C2r] have speculated wildly about this with reference to that verse of *Satire* 6 by Juvenal:

> *when the Aemilian bridge nearby offers itself to you?*[87]

This bridge had previously been called Sublicius.[88] After it was damaged by the Tiber's floods, it was restored by Tiberius Caesar.

---

85. The Pons Sublicius was located south of the Tiber Island, in correspondence to the modern Piazza Bocca della Verità. It is no longer standing, but its name has been inherited by the modern Ponte Sublicio, which is located further south and connects Piazza dell'Emporio in Testaccio with Porta Portese. According to ancient sources, it was the most ancient, wooden bridge of Rome, built by King Ancus Marcius (Liv. 1.33.6; Plin. *Nat.* 36.23.100). It was considered sacred and, according to the sources, it had to be rebuilt in wood, also for practical reasons so that in time of war it could be easily removed (Dion. Hal. 9.68.2). For a history of the bridge, see Filippo Coarelli, "Pons Sublicius," LTUR 4:113; and Rabun Taylor, "Tiber River Bridges and the Development of the Ancient City of Rome," *The Waters of Rome* 2 (June 2002): 3–4, at: https://waters.iath.virginia.edu/first.html.

86. P. Victor, Pomponio Leto, Fabrizio Varano, Flavio Biondo, *De urbe Roma scribentes*. Flavio Biondo, *De locis ac civitatibus Italiae, deque eius appellationibus priscis ac novis* (Bologna: Girolamo Benedetti, 1520), 53.

87. Juv. 6.30. See *Satirae cum commentis Antonii Mancinelli, Domitii Calderini, Georgii Vallae* (Nuremberg: Anton Koberger, 1497), fol. 66r. In their commentary on *Satire* 6, these authors comment that the Pons Aemilius is also called "Pons Milvius." This assertion may be the source of Gómez's comment that they speculate "wildly."

88. Gómez seems to be conflating the Pons Aemilius and the Pons Sublicius. The Pons Sublicius was a wooden bridge (see above n. 85), while the Pons Aemilius was a stone bridge that acquired several names over the

Then, Antoni[n]us Pius rebuilt it in marble, because of which it has been called "marble bridge" to today. It was destroyed a second time under [Pope] Hadrian I,[89] and its remains can still be seen at that place on the Tiber's banks where ships from everywhere import wine for sale [Fig. 5].[90] Therefore, it is clear that it was no small amount of water that destroyed that bridge, which had been built with very solid bases and arches.

The second of the two bridges that collapsed is believed to be the one that we see ruined at Porta Trionfale, near the church of Sto. Spirito. It was called the Vatican Bridge or, according to Flavius

centuries: Pons Lepidus, Pons Lapideus, Pons Senatus, and in Gómez's time, Ponte Sta. Maria. It was the first stone bridge of the city, north of the Pons Sublicius. According to ancient sources, it was built starting from 179 BCE (pillars) by M. Fulvius Nobilior, who was censor with M. Aemilius Lepidus (Liv. 40.51.4). However, its existence can date back to 241 BCE, when the via Aurelia was constructed. Therefore, the bridge built in 179 BCE was probably a reconstruction linked to the restoration of the Portus Tiberinus. It was often damaged by floods and was repaired many times. In the sixteenth century, it was partially destroyed in the flood of 1557, repaired for the Jubilee of 1575, and then finally destroyed in the flood of 1598. Two of the three remaining arches were removed during the construction of the Tiber embankment walls in the 1880s. A single arch of the bridge remains south of the Tiber Island and is known as the "Ponte Rotto," i.e., "broken bridge." For the ancient bridge, see Filippo Coarelli, "Pons Aemilius," LTUR 4:106–7; and Taylor, "Tiber River Bridges," 4–5. For sixteenth-century repairs, see Claudia Conforti, "Il cantiere di Michelangelo al Ponte Sta. Maria a Roma (1548–49)," in *I ponti delle capitali d'Europa dal Corno d'Oro alla Senna*, Donatella Calabi and Claudia Conforti, ed. (Milan: Electa, 2002), 75–87; D'Onofrio, *Il Tevere*, 141–65; David Karmon, *Ruin of the Eternal City: Antiquity and Preservation in Renaissance Rome* (New York: Oxford University Press, 2011), 170–98; and Long, *Engineering the Eternal City*, 93–95 and 99–102.

89. See the account of the sixteenth flood, pp. 54–55 below.

90. The Portus Tiberinus occupied the area on the left bank of the river, north of the temple of Portunus. While the area was a natural landing place even earlier, in 179 BCE the censor M. Aemilius Lepidus built structures and a wall that limited the area of the port and restored the bridge linked to it. See Carlo Buzzetti, "Portus Tiberinus," LTUR 4:155–56.

Fig. 5. View of Pons Aemilius, now Ponte Rotto. Drawing by Gerard Ter Borch the Elder, ink on paper, 16[09?]. Courtesy of the Rijksmuseum, Amsterdam.

Josephus in book 7 of *The Jewish War,* the Triumphal Bridge, as only nobles used to pass over it. Its foundations, which are extant, clearly show how soundly constructed that bridge was. Yet they were not so well built that they were able to resist the violence of such a great flood.[91] Nevertheless, the bridge of Hadrian, which today is called Ponte Sant'Angelo, was able to manage those onslaughts because it was the strongest among all the structures that men have built[92]

---

91. Pons Neronianus, otherwise called Vatican Bridge or Pons Triumphalis. Its remains are still visible in low water south of Ponte Vittorio Emanuele II, in front of Sto. Spirito. It was probably built at the time of Caligula to link the city with his circus and the *horti Agrippinae,* which were on the right bank of the Tiber. See Paolo Liverani, "Pons Neronianus," LTUR 4:111; David R. Marshall, "Piranesi, Juvarra, and the Triumphal Bridge Tradition," *The Art Bulletin* 85.2 (2003): 321–52; and Taylor, "Tiber River Bridges," 11–13.

92. The ancient Pons Aelius, now called Ponte Sant'Angelo, was built by Emperor Hadrian in 134 CE in front of his mausoleum (Castel Sant'Angelo) to connect it with the Campus Martius. See Francesca de Caprariis, "Pons Aelius," LTUR 4:105–6; Taylor, "Tiber River Bridges," 12–14; and Mark Weil, *The History and Decoration of the Ponte S. Angelo* (University Park: Pennsylvania State University Press, 1974).

Fig. 6. Castel Sant'Angelo and Ponte Sant'Angelo in foreground. Detail of View of Rome from Hartmann von Schedel, Registrum huius Operis libri cronicarum cum figuris et ymagibus ab inicio mundi [Nuremberg Chronicle]. Nuremberg: Anton Hoberger, 1493. Woodcut created by Michael Wolgemut and Michael Pleydenwurff. Courtesy of The Met Museum.

[Fig. 6]. In book 10, chapter 8 of *On the Art of Building*, however, Alberti questioned whether its construction could further withstand the Tiber floods. For each year the floods burden the pillars with troublesome trunks and branches that they seize from the fields and render the mouths of the arches mostly blocked. In this situation it happens that, as the waters rise, the waves swirl together and crash down on each other; this undermines the pillars from behind and severely compromises the structure of the bridge."[93] This according to Alberti.

Indeed, we saw this prediction come true with the latest flood of the Tiber. Because the two arches beneath the citadel of Sant'Angelo had become blocked, the waters accumulated in this latest flood struck with great force and attacked it as if they were an army arrayed for battle. As a result, once part of the structure was destroyed, almost the entire bridge was shaken to its foundation along with the adjacent buildings belonging to private persons.[94] The bridge to the Janiculum, or Pons Aurelius, which is now called Ponte Sisto, suffered almost the same attack with the same damage.[95] Its arches were more extended and larger than the others and therefore they were able to manage a great quantity of water. Nonetheless, in this

93. Leon Battista Alberti, *On the Art of Building in Ten Books*, Joseph Rykwert, Neil Leach, and Robert Tavernor, trans. (Cambridge, MA: MIT Press, 1988), 346 (10.10); and Leon Battista Alberti, *L'Architettura [De re aedificatoria]*, Giovanni Orlandi, ed. and trans.; Paolo Portoghesi, intro and notes, 2 vols. (Milan: Edizione il Polifilo, 1966), 2:948–49 (10.10). Alberti discusses bridge building in detail in book 4.6, where he describes building pillars like "a Liburnian galley" (a light ship built with lumber from Liburnia in Dalmatia with a pointed prow and stern). The pointed stern, called a cutwater, is described here. See Alberti, *On the Art of Building*, 107–13, esp. 110, and 382, n. 86; and Alberti, *L'Architettura [De re aedificatoria]*, 308–23, esp. 314–15. This is a good description of "scouring." See Hamill, *Bridge Hydraulics*, 15–17.

94. Gómez discusses the blocking of the Ponte Sant'Angelo in greater detail in his description of the flood of 1530. See below, pp. 65–66 n. 148.

95. Ponte Sisto, which connects the rione Regola with Piazza Trilussa, was constructed on an ancient bridge called Pons Aurelius and is also identified with the Pons Agrippae. This bridge was built to connect the properties of M. Vipsanius Agrippa on the two banks of the Tiber and to lead a secondary branch of the Acqua Vergine to Trastevere. See Filippo Coarelli, "Pons Agrippae, Pons Aurelius, Pons Valentiniani," LTUR 4:107–8; D'Onofrio, *Il Tevere*, 203–25; Long, *Engineering the Eternal City*, 95–98; Minou Schraven, "Founding Rome Anew: Pope Sixtus IV and the Foundation of the Ponte Sisto, 1473," in *Foundation, Dedication, and Consecration in Early Modern Europe*, Maarten Delbeke and Minou Schraven, ed. (London: Brill, 2012), 129–51; and Taylor, "Tiber River Bridges," 10–11.

latest flood, which we witnessed during the reign of Pope Clement VII, there was so much water and such great force that there can be no doubt that it would have taken the [entire] bridge with it, had the water not created a passage for itself by tearing up the foundations of the bridge on the left side. We shall speak about this flood later in its own place. It is enough to have demonstrated by its effects that that flood was greater than all the others in magnitude and in the amount of water. [C2v]

Seventh flood [44–43 BCE]

Great and unusual was the flood that is remembered to have happened under Augustus. As Enea Silvio [Piccolomini][96] records in his letter 103 (when he describes the rise of the Danube), at this time the Tiber overflowed the Etruscan bank and reached the monuments of King Numa Pompilius and the temples of Vesta. If we trust the words of Horace *Odes* 2, there was no greater flood of the Tiber.[97] Therefore, we must think that Augustus, although preoccupied by far greater concerns, directed his mind to this matter alone. Indeed, as [Suetonius] Tranquillus reports, "he improved the city, which was vulnerable to floods, and widened the riverbed of the Tiber to control floods."[98]

Eighth flood [15 CE]

The flood that occurred under Emperor Tiberius [r.14–37 CE], however, was no less significant. For, as Tacitus says in book 1, in

---

96. Enea Silvio Piccolomini, *Epistolae familiares* 103 (Milan: Ulrich Scinzenzeler, A. Archinto, J. Vinzalio, 1497), f. 42r.

97. Hor. *Carm.* 1.2.1–20. Here Gómez refers to the Regia (the residence of the king), the Domus Publica (the residence of the *pontifex maximus*), and the temple of Vesta, all three of which, according to ancient sources, were built in the Roman Forum by the second king of Rome, Numa Pompilius. The Regia has been identified as the small trapezoidal building between the temple of Julius, the temple of Antoninus and Faustina, and the temple of Vesta. For the Regia, see Russell T. Scott, "Regia," LTUR 4:189–92; for the Domus Publica, idem, "Domus Publica," LTUR 1:165–66; and for the Temple of Vesta, idem, "Vesta, aedes," LTUR 5:125–28. See also Aldrete, *Floods*, 21–23.

98. Suet. *Aug.* 3. See also Marsico, *Il Tevere*, 93–94.

that year the Tiber, enlarged by continuous downpours, brought great destruction to people and buildings, so that it caused trouble for almost all of Italy.[99] We mentioned this earlier, in book 1.[100]

Floods after the Coming of Christ[101]

Ninth flood [69 CE]
Among the major floods of the Tiber, we should also report the one that [Suetonius] Tranquillus mentions in the life of Otho, which blocked access to the city with debris from buildings up to the twentieth milestone.[102] At that time, Linus was the pope [r.c.67–76 CE]. From this time on, we will recount floods under the names of the popes. For the light of the Christian religion, Christ, had now arisen. From him, just as from a new beginning of the world, we shall begin our count of the years, so that in this way the matter can be perceived and understood more clearly.

Tenth flood[103]
At the time of Pope Anacletus [r.88–91 CE] the Tiber rose immensely and demolished many buildings. Indeed, this flood foretold many evils. For in many places there followed earthquakes, famine, and pestilence. Emperor Trajan [r.98–117 CE] sought out remedies from all quarters and confronted and relieved these evils as much as he could. According to Rivail's testimony, he later established that:

> houses should not exceed sixty feet in height, because, if ever such events happened [again], they would collapse easily, and expenses would be too great.[104]

---

99. Tac. *Ann.* 1.76, 1.79. See also Aldrete, *Floods*, 25–26.

100. See above, pp. 34–35 n. 58.

101. This division seems to be based on the date of Christ's crucifixion rather than that of his birth.

102. Suet. *Otho* 8. 3. See also Aldrete, *Floods*, 26–27.

103. See Ps. Aurelius Victor, *Caesares* 13.12; Plin. *Ep.* 8.17.2. Modern scholars believe that this flood occurred during the reign of Trajan but cannot date it more precisely. See Aldrete, *Floods*, 28–29.

104. Aymar du Rivail, *Civilis Historiae Iuris, sive in duodecim Tabularum Leges Commentariorum libri quinque* (Mainz: Schoeffer, 1527), 4:233.

Eleventh flood [under the reign of Hadrian][105]
The [flood] that in the time of Emperor Hadrian [r.117–38 CE] was accompanied by so many evils can be listed among the memorable floods. [This is] not so much on account of the violence of the waters as on the occurrence of calamitous events at the same time. [C3r] For, as Aelius Spartianus records in the *Life [of Hadrian]*,[106] at that time, along with the Tiber's flooding there were famines and pestilence that devastated many cities. In fact, this flood happened in the years between 119 and 129 CE, between the pontificate of Alexander I [r.105–15] and Sixtus I [r.115–25], first popes of Rome. For, when Emperor Hadrian was still alive, these two popes, elected one after the other, died.

Twelfth flood [147 CE]
In the same category, however, the accumulation of water that Julius Capitolinus discusses in the *[Life] of Antoninus Pius*[107] can appear more violent. It was foretold by previous omens as the beginning of greater prodigies. Preceding that flood there occurred a famine, the collapse of the Circus [Maximus],[108] an earthquake, and a fire in which 340 insulae and houses in Rome were destroyed, along with the city of Narbonne, the city of Antioch, and the forum of Carthage, which burned at the same time. Indeed, after the flood of the Tiber, a comet appeared, a child with two heads [was born], and a woman gave birth to five children at the same time.[109] In Arabia an unusually large-crested snake[110] was seen devouring half of itself starting at the tail. And in that time, barley growing on top of trees spread terror. Accompanied by such and so many prodigies, the flood therefore deserves to be remembered. In the year 139 CE, when this flood of

---

105. See Aldrete, *Floods*, 29–30.

106. SHA *Hadr.* 21.5–6.

107. SHA *Ant.* 9.1–3. See also Aldrete, *Floods*, 30.

108. Ancient sources report that under Antoninus Pius the upper section of the circus collapsed causing the death of 1,112 spectators. See Valentini and Zucchetti, ed., "Chronograph of 354," in *Codice Topografico*, 1:276; SHA *Ant.* 9.1.

109. du Rivail, *Civilis Historiae Iuris*, 237.

110. SHA *Ant.* 9.1–5.

the Tiber happened, Pope Telesphorus [r.125–36 CE] occupied the see of Peter, as Platina says.[111]

Thirteenth flood [161–62 CE]
We should also not neglect that overflow of the Tiber that the same Julius Capitolinus reports in the *[Life of] Marcus [Aurelius] Antoni[n]us* [r.161–80 CE], which disturbed the emperor's happiness and security.[112] For that flood was very severe and brought great damage to the buildings of the city and to animals. Thereafter famines, very harsh wars, and pestilence followed, so that corpses were carried away on carriages and wagons. If the pious and magnanimous prince had not confronted these evils, the same author would have gone on at greater length about the city in more than just one passage. Yet, it should be observed that the historical writing of those times was very uneven and sloppy. For neither Damasus nor Platina, who very diligently put together the history of the popes, record this flood or the great number of prodigies that happened at the same time. In any case, this flood occurred between 160 and 168 CE.

Fourteenth flood [589 CE]
But who could pass over with dry eyes the disaster recounted by so many authors that the [C3v] Tiber's flood inflicted at the time of Pope Pelagius II [r.579–90]? Indeed, in book 18, Paul the Deacon reports that during those times there were such severe floods in so many places that people believed that the deluge of Noah was happening again.[113] For in the territories of Venice[114] and of Liguria, and in other Italian regions as well, estates became lagoons, many people and animals died, roads were destroyed, streets were devastated. At

---

111. Gómez's error in chronology here stems from his use of Platina, who credits Telesphorus with the restoration of the city after this flood. See Platina, *Platynae historici Liber*, 2.

112. SHA *Marc.* 8.4–5. See also Aldrete, *Floods*, 30–31.

113. Paul the Deacon, *Historia Langobardorum* 3.23–24, L. Bethmann and G. Waitz, ed., MGH, *Scriptores Rerum Langobardarum* (Hanover: Hahn, 1878), 104; and see Aldrete, *Floods*, 29–30.

114. Venice was often designated with the plural *Venetiae* because the polity was originally composed of communities spread across multiple islands in the lagoon.

the same time, the Adige River rose so much that around the basilica of San Zeno the Martyr, which is situated outside of the walls of the city of Verona, the water reached the upper windows. Despite this, the water barely penetrated inside, as blessed Gregory, who later [became] pope [Gregory I], wrote in book 3 of the *Dialogues*.[115] The walls of the city of Verona were also destroyed for the most part by the same flood. They say that that flood portended the lamentable burning of the city of Verona, which followed thereafter.

The same author continues [saying that] in this great profusion of floods, the Tiber River rose so much in Rome that its water flowed over the walls of the city and occupied the most elevated regions. Then, along with many snakes, a dragon of great and wondrous size, after passing through the city through this riverbed, descended to the sea. [These serpents were] drowned by the waves of the sea and pushed back to the shores. They infected the surrounding regions with their stench, as the archbishop of Florence reports more fully in his life of Gregory.[116] From the rotting of the snakes and the dragon, and from the vaporous stench of the waters and mud dispersed through low-lying areas of the city, such a severe pestilence followed that people died from sneezing.[117] It so afflicted the people that barely a tenth survived out of such a great and inestimable multitude. First of all, it struck and immediately killed Pope Pelagius [II; r.578–90], an especially venerable man. Barely anyone would have survived amidst such a severe and sad persecution, had Gregory, who was then elected pope

---

115. Gregory I, *Dialogi* III.19, PL 77, cols. 268C–269C.

116. Gómez's reference here is uncertain, but he seems to refer to the *Life* of Gregory I now attributed to Paul the Deacon (c.720–c.798) and edited in PL 75, cols. 42–64. The relevant passage occurs at *Vita* 10, cols. 45D–46B. This story is repeated verbatim by Jacobus de Voragine, *Legenda Aurea*, Alessandro Brovarone and Lucetta Vitale Brovarone, ed. (Milan: Einaudi 2007), 234; Jacobus de Voragine, *The Golden Legend: Readings on the Saints*, William Granger Ryan, trans. (Princeton, NJ: Princeton University Press, 1993), 1:171–84, at 173 for the flood.

117. Sneezing (*sternutatio*) was also one of the symptoms of the plague of Athens recounted by Thucydides (Th. 2.49). We have not been able to find explicit reference to "sneezing" in any of the sources on Gregory I.

with the consent of all,[118] not responded with prayers, sackcloth, and the sevenfold litany.[119] For, on the very day on which the supplications were performed, eighty people suddenly died in the space of only one hour. It would take too long to enumerate the unheard-of prodigies of those times, which the above-mentioned authors describe at length in connection with this disaster. In any case, as Palmieri writes in the continuation of the *Chronicle* by Eusebius [of Caesarea], this flood happened in the year of Christian salvation 586, and according to others, 576.[120] Indeed, as they affirm in the book called *Fasciculus temporum*[121] (if we can completely trust it), more terrifying and wondrous prodigies occurred all at once [in Rome] in a single age than have occurred since the world began.

----

118. Jacobus de Voragine, *Legenda Aurea*, 234. Gregory I was pope 590–604.

119. An account of this procession, the *litania settiforme* — called "sevenfold" because it involved all the citizens divided into seven groups — is contained, along with a description of the plague, in Gregory of Tours, *Historiae Francorum* 10.1, Bruno Krusch and Wilhelm Levison, ed., MGH, *Scriptores Rerum Merovingicarum* (Hanover: Hahn, 1951), 1:477–81.

120. Matteo Palmieri (1406–75) was the author of the *Liber de Temporibus*, a universal chronology from the birth of Christ to 1448, which is also referred to as the continuation of the *Chronicles* of Eusebius of Caesarea. For the flood of 586, see Matteo Palmieri, *Liber de Temporibus*, Gino Scaramella, ed., RIS 26.1 (Città di Castello: S. Lapi, 1906–15), 60. This Matteo Palmieri is not to be confused with his almost namesake Mattia Palmieri, who was Neapolitan and was the author of the last part of the continuation of the *Chronicles* of Eusebius (up to 1482). See Elena Valeri, "Palmieri, Matteo," DBI 80 (2014): 614–18. For this flood, see also Marsico, *Il Tevere*, 94.

121. The popular historical compendium, *Fasciculus temporum* by the Carthusian monk Werner Rolevinck, was first published in 1474. It went through forty editions before Rolevinck's death in 1502 and continued to be printed and modified into the eighteenth century. The passage about "*mirabilia*," as Rolevinck calls them, is in the life of Pelagius II, just before the life of Gregory I. Most editions we have seen do not have contemporary foliation or pagination; but see Werner Rolevinck, *Fasciculus temporum omnes antiquorum cronicas complectens* (Strasbourg: Johan Prüss [not before 1490]), fol. LVIIr–v.

Fifteenth flood [716][122]

Under Pope Gregory II in the year 717 from the Virgin birth, [C4r] when the emperor was still Theodosius [III, r.715–17] according to the calculation of the Florentine Palmieri,[123] the Tiber burst into the city through the Porta Flaminia[124] with an unusual surge. As Platina writes, it brought great damage to the city and its inhabitants for seven days.[125] After destroying houses and uprooting trees, the water rushed through the city like a dense battle line and filled all the low-lying areas. It rose so much that on the via Lata[126] it exceeded the height of a man. It grew so deep that it was possible to go in small boats from Ponte Milvio up to the steps of St. Peter's. It was a harsh event and more disastrous for those who did not foresee it. Indeed, it could be judged to be more bitter because that flood, as if aided by heaven, had been foretold by a manifest prodigy. For a comet had been seen in the sky beforehand pointing its tail toward the north; and at the time of this flood the moon eclipsed and appeared blood red until midnight. Therefore, if we follow Damasus, we should rightly believe that this flood went over the walls of the city.[127] For this reason Gregory took pity on the Christians for these horrible calamities and performed supplications throughout the city to appease the wrath of God.

Sixteenth flood [792]

Another unusual flood of the Tiber happened during the twentieth year [of the papacy] of Pope Hadrian I [r.772–95]. For the river cascaded like a torrent through Porta Flaminia, which now is

---

122. According to modern scholarship, the date of the flood is 716. See Aldrete, *Floods*, 243. This and other floods to 1277 are also briefly discussed by Marsico, *Il Tevere*, 94–98.

123. Palmieri, *Liber de Temporibus*, 69.

124. I.e., Porta del Popolo, in the homonymous piazza. It was one of the ancient gates opened in the Aurelian Wall and took its original name from the via Flaminia, which began there. For the ancient gate, see Giuseppina Pisani Sartorio, "Porta Flaminia," LTUR 3:303–4.

125. Platina, *Platynae historici Liber*, 123.

126. Today, via del Corso.

127. Duchesne, ed., *Liber Pontificalis*, 1:390.

called Porta del Popolo, and toppled the gate itself to the ground, as Damasus and Platina write.[128] Spreading in every direction, it then destroyed for the second time the Pons Sublicius (which we said had collapsed during another flood and which M. Anoni[n]us Pius had rebuilt in marble),[129] along with great loss of life and goods. Moreover, it destroyed many buildings of the city, animals, trees, fields, and caused most of the city walls and towers to collapse. [The city], which had been supported by [goods coming on] river boats, almost fell into extreme poverty. By papal decree, food was distributed with these [boats] to the poor who were unable to go out and otherwise lacked all care. That cataclysm caused harm not only in the short term but was also the reason why Rome suffered in the following year from a shortage of grain. Pope Hadrian comforted the city affected by such misfortune by donating much to many people so they might suffer less from this calamity. He rebuilt the city walls and towers [that had been] destroyed by the violence of the waters. What more? Amidst such extreme poverty, Hadrian did everything that the best of princes would have done.

Seventeenth flood [860]
It is reported that the Tiber also flooded the entire city in an extraordinary manner under Pope Nicholas I [r.858–67]. For [the river] so filled the entire plain that extends from the via Lata to the Tarpeian Rock and from the via Argentaria[130] to the Aventine [C4v] that it was believed that the Flood [of Noah] was beginning. During this flood, some famous places were devastated by the force of the water, as some reported. Many houses were also destroyed, everywhere trees and crops were swept away. This did not happen only once in that year, as Platina says. In the month of December, Rome suffered a second flood.[131] The pope, striving to remedy and

128. Platina, *Platynae historici Liber*, 138. "Damasus" here refers to the *Liber Pontificalis*.

129. See Sixth flood, pp. 42–48.

130. Here Gómez seems to refer to the divus Argentarius, the ancient street that runs on the slopes of the Capitoline Hill between the Roman Forum and the back of the Vittoriano. See Carlo Buzzetti and Giuseppina Pisani Sartorio, "Clivus Argentarius," LTUR 1:280.

131. Platina, *Platynae historici Liber*, 153.

mitigate this damage, did not omit any kind of service and [act of] piety. Yet the pope was exhausted by the very great expense and troubles of these events as well as by the great fear and novelty of previous prodigies, and therefore he could not accomplish what he had intended. For, according to Palmieri,[132] two horrifying prodigies preceded that flood. It is said that in Brescia it rained blood for three days. In Gaul, a great swarm of six-legged locusts arose and occupied everything in a repulsive way, until they were pushed toward the British Sea by the force of the wind and died submerged by the waves. Then, the current of the sea pushed them back toward the shore and they infected the air with their stench. Once that tract of land was corrupted, there followed a pestilence and a great famine so that almost a third of the population died. These misfortunes happened around the year of the Lord 862, even though Matteo Palmieri had ascribed them to the time of Hadrian II [r.867–72].[133]

Eighteenth flood [1230]

The force of the water that the Tiber inflicted on the city at the time of Gregory IX [r.1227–41] was also severe and very bitter, as Damasus, Platina, and Sabellicus report.[134] Rising beyond measure, [the Tiber] inflicted great damage on mortals. Soon after there followed such a horrible and dire pestilence that barely a tenth of the population survived. For vital spirits, consumed by putrefaction and diseased blood, abandoned sweet souls. A solar prodigy accompanied these evils: a greater eclipse than ever before recorded.

132. Palmieri, *Liber de Temporibus*, 79. For Matteo Palmieri see p. 53 n. 120.

133. Palmieri, *Liber de Temporibus*, 79, in his continuation of the *Chronicles* of Eusebius.

134. Platina, *Platynae historici Liber*, 232; Marcantonio Sabellico, *Posterior pars eiusdem Rapsodie historiaru[m] M. Antonio Coccij Sabellici contine[n]s sex Enneades reliquas cu[m] earunde[m] repertorijs et epitomis* (Paris: Jehan Petit, 1513), fol. 245v. The reference to Damasus in the *Liber Pontificalis* likely refers to the so-called "Life" of Gregory IX where there is a full account of the flood and the pope's response. For discussion of the text's history and a critical edition, see Alberto Spataro, ed., *Velud fulgor meridianus: La 'Vita' di Papa Gregorio IX. Edizione, traduzione, e commento*, Ordines 8 (Milan: Vita e Pensiero, 2018), c.13, 92.

Then there followed some difficult and hostile disputes between the pope and the Romans, which made that age sad and most bitter, as historians describe extensively.[135]

Nineteenth flood [1277]
Among the prodigious floods of the Tiber, [historians] also record the one that is said to have foretold the death of Pope Nicholas III [r.1277–80] in the prophecy made from the rise of the Tiber, according to Platina.[136] For during this time the Tiber rose in a very unusual way and was so swollen that at the Pantheon, which is now the church of the Virgin Mother of God, the floodwaters of the river flowed over the great altar by more than four feet. This was the year of Salvation 1280.[137] Foretold by a prodigy, the death of Nicholas III followed. For when [the pope] died suddenly — although very restrained in his eating and drinking and alien to pleasure — [Dr] it was believed that the vast, destructive flooding of the Tiber had foretold it.

Twentieth flood [November 30, 1422]
It was the year 1421[138] of the Christian salvation when Pope Martin V [r.1417–31] directed his gaze to the appearance of this wretched

---

135. For Gregory IX's struggles with the Romans and especially the Annibaldi, see Platina, *Platynae historici Liber*, 232; Sabellico, *Posterior pars*, fol. 245v. One of the best, if partial, witnesses to the controversies between pope and Roman nobility is the so-called "Life" of Gregory IX, Spataro, ed., esp. c.18, 100. See also Robert Brentano, *Rome Before Avignon: A Social History of Thirteenth-Century Rome* (New York: Basic Books, 1974), 107; Paolo Brezzi, *Roma e l'impero medioevale (774–1252)*, Storia di Roma 10 (Bologna: Licinio Cappelli, 1947), 408–25; and Ovidio Capitani, "Gregorio IX," DBI 59 (2002): 166–78. For the (no longer extant) markers that had been placed to measure the height of this flood, see Giuseppe Scalia, "*Turbidus Tiber*: In margine ad alcune antiche epigrafi su inondazioni tiberine," in *Studi in onore di Leopoldo Sandri* (Rome: Ministero per i beni culturali e ambientali 1950), 3:873–79. These markers, however, are not mentioned by Gómez.

136. Platina, *Platynae historici Liber*, 250.

137. The flood occurred on November 6, 1277. See Aldrete, *Floods*, 244.

138. The flood occurred on November 30, 1422. See Aldrete, *Floods*, 244. For discussions of Roman floods of the fifteenth and sixteenth centuries, see

city. It had long been devastated by schismatic insurrections, by the fury of tyrants, by hunger, war, and pestilence. For everywhere there was squalor, sacred buildings were crumbling into the muck, there was great desolation, streets looked muddy and squalid, and a sort of wild and barbarous harshness had invaded the city. As a result, [the pope] was welcomed with huge acclamation by everyone and carefully worked so that soon everything could change for the better. Everything was already in a happy state and had been restored to its former splendor when around St. Andrew's Day [November 30] the Tiber burst into the city from Porta Flaminia and flooded the entire surface of the city, inflicted severe damage on the citizens, and reopened old wounds. The violence of those waters weakened two days later, but many animals were swept away by that flood. The height of this flood can be seen today near the temple of [Sta. Maria sopra] Minerva on a marker inscribed with [its] record [Fig 7].

Twenty-first Flood [January 8, 1476][139]
Sixtus IV [r.1471–85] had been pope for several years already, when, after much civic unrest, the Tiber overflowed its banks in the month of November and brought great damage to those who lived nearby. Many animals drowned in this flood. Afterwards there was a severe pestilence caused by their putrefaction. Then, according to Vincentius and more recent authors,[140] there occurred such horrendous and astonishing prodigies as could scarcely be believed. [There were] also winds so powerful that many buildings were destroyed. All these things portended the death of the pope.

Twenty-second Flood [December 5, 1495]
It was the second year from the election of Alexander VI [r.1492–1503] when the Alpine rivers, as if conspiring, swelled prodigiously and flooded almost all the land between the River Po and the Alps, region by region, with great destruction of people and death of

---

Esposito, "Roma e i suoi 'diluvi,'" 5–26; idem, "Le inondazioni del Tevere"; and Long, "Responses to a Recurrent Disaster," forthcoming.

139. Gómez places this flood in November, but according to a now lost flood marker, the flood occurred on January 8, 1476. See Di Martino, Di Martino, and Belati, *Huc Tiber ascendit*, 179.

140. We have not been able to identify this Vincentius.

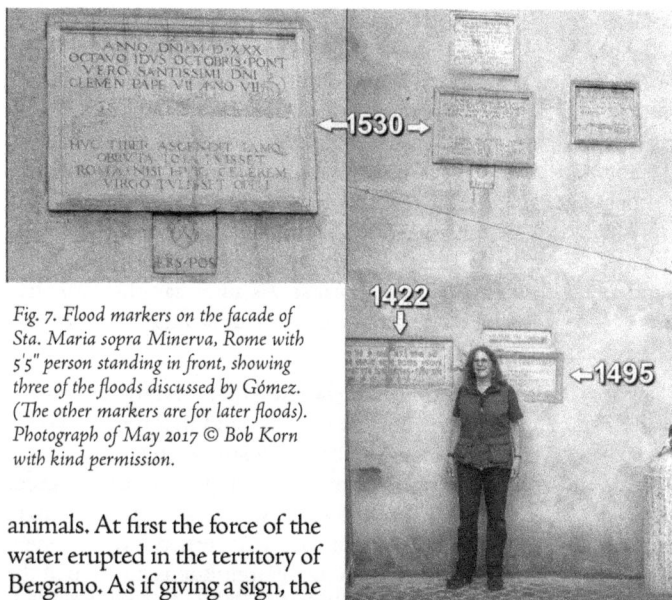

Fig. 7. Flood markers on the facade of Sta. Maria sopra Minerva, Rome with 5'5" person standing in front, showing three of the floods discussed by Gómez. (The other markers are for later floods). Photograph of May 2017 © Bob Korn with kind permission.

animals. At first the force of the water erupted in the territory of Bergamo. As if giving a sign, the flooding of the Adige affected all that region that surrounds Verona with the same destructive power. That was not the end of the damage, however, for then the powerful flood invaded the territory of Padua and the whole region of the Carni.[141] Not much longer after that, the Tiber, exceedingly swollen, flooded the whole plain of the city up to the foot of the hills. As a result, in the church of San Giacomo degli Spagnoli[142] the water was higher than a man, as we can read on the marble inscription. From this flood Rome suffered very great damage, [Dv] and many buildings collapsed with the violence of the water.

But in the center of this very opulent city, such a flood, although powerful, did not even disturb the minds of the inhabitants. For Rome was full of gold everywhere, and already it could not sustain its greatness. Therefore, amidst such excessive wealth, amidst such an

---

141. The people of Carnia, a region in northeastern Italy in the area of Friuli in the province of Udine.

142. A church in Piazza Navona.

abundance of all things, the flood was quite fitting and opportune, as [is] a phlebotomy when there is too much unhealthy and fat blood. For it is usual that favorable and excessively abundant things bring humans far away from themselves and, since they do not understand themselves, they neglect and disregard the Savior of all things. Therefore, the flood was good because it forced people to come to their senses. Just as if touched by the goad of misfortune, [they were forced] to recognize what is true and just. Nevertheless, these floods had something more astonishing, namely that they occurred suddenly with very little evident cause. As some say, the rivers had not even swelled because of rain, and this devastation spread with not even an interval of one day.

I know that there are some who believed that this huge amount of water had come from the rains in the Alps and that the tree leaves, knocked down by the wind, had caused many streams to suddenly cascade down into the rivers below, producing an unusual rise [of the water level]. But whether the cause was this, or another more hidden, the unusual appearance of the event turned into a prodigy. Many traced this prodigious flood to the tumultuous invasion of the French into Italy, at which time both Alfonso II lost the kingdom of Naples and his father Ferdinand died while preparing for war.[143] Others linked [the flood] to other causes. There are also those who blame the Tiber flood on the earliest years of [Pope] Alexander.[144] Indeed, this will give [us] very little difficulty if we consider the inscriptions in multiple places in Rome. For a travertine stone on the church of San Giacomo from the year 1495 from the birth of

---

143. The king of France, Charles VIII, invaded Italy on September 2, 1494. Ferdinand I (Ferdinando, Ferrante), king of Naples (r.1458–94) had died on January 25, 1494, about seven months before. Whereupon his son, Alfonso II (r.1494–95), became king of Naples. Charles' army entered and conquered Naples on February 22, 1495. See David Abulafia, ed., *The French Descent into Renaissance Italy, 1494–1495: Antecedents and Effects* (Aldershot: Variorum, 1995); Christine Shaw and Michael Mallett, *The Italian Wars, 1494–1559*, 2nd rev. ed. (New York: Routledge, 2018), 6–41; and Charlotte Nichols and James H. Mc Gregor, ed., *Renaissance Naples: A Documentary History, 1400–1600* (New York: Italica Press, 2019), 2–24, 53–92, et passim.

144. Pope Alexander VI (r.1492–1503).

Christ, on the 5th of December, records that a flood happened more or less in the second year of Alexander's [papacy].[145]

Twenty-Third Flood [October 8, 1530]
When I had greater leisure, I was going to describe that wretched injury accompanied by many disasters that the flooding of the Tiber inflicted in the year of salvation 1530. But the cares and daily business of public duties were keeping me busy and absolutely overwhelmed and were growing day by day. It would therefore come to pass that, if I postponed this project to another time, I would possibly have even less time. Therefore, while the memory of so great an evil is fresh, while [D2r] my mind is still in mourning over this calamity, I considered it worthwhile to summarize this matter as completely as possible [Figs. 8 and 9a–b].

Dawn had broken on that unspeakable day of Saturday, which was the eighth of the month of October. Then the Tiber, displaced from its usual bed, brought into the city mountains of water to the great amazement and injury of all. For it seemed that on that one day all the elements had conspired with each other. Great fear caused by the groan of collapsing buildings wore out gentle souls. Furthermore, the memory of past evil struck the hearts of the wretched, scars of which were still fresh.[146] At once some claimed that God had sent this flood to avenge sins. They justified their claims with certain signs, namely that under a clear sky and without any prior downpours, such a huge force of water burst forth that it almost seemed as if the waters of the abyss had been released. They added that there was an eclipse of the sun and the moon that happened at the same degree [of latitude] on the same day as the flood.[147] But others attributed it to the natural cycle of [celestial]

---

145. *Nonae decembris* = December 5. For the inscriptions around Rome reporting the 1495 Tiber River flood, see Di Martino, Di Martino, and Belati, *Huc Tiber Ascendit*, 50–54; and Scalia, "*Turbidus Tiber*," 886–95.

146. This is a reference to the Sack of Rome, which occurred in 1527, for which, see pp. 7–8 n. 8.

147. The dates of all solar and lunar eclipses are known. The closest solar eclipse to the flood of October 8, 1530 was on September 21, 1530, and the closest lunar eclipse was on September 28, 1530. See NASA Eclipse

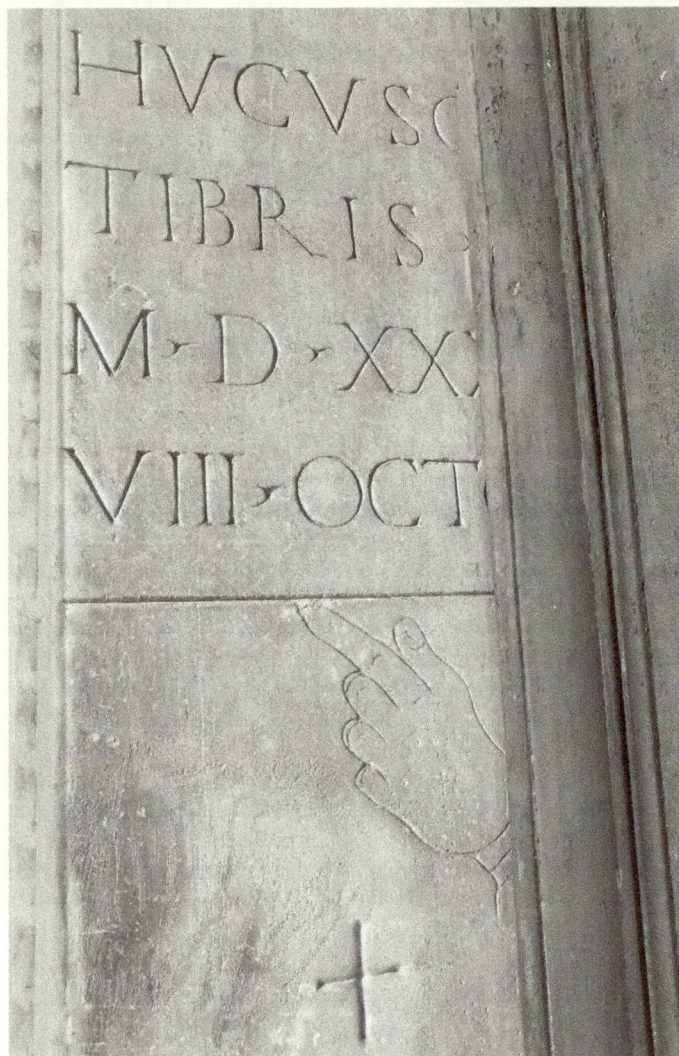

Fig. 8. Flood marker for the 1530 flood located on the door frame of Sta. Maria della Pace. Photograph of December 2022 © Chiara Bariviera with kind permission.

bodies. At the same time, as some have reported very recently, they also remembered the flood that happened naturally throughout the entire world at the time of [Pope] Benedict XII [r.1334–42]. At that time, without any previous rain, the earth spontaneously issued torrents of gushing flood water as if its veins had burst. These torrents are reported to have caused nearly infinite damage. So now, rejecting the lunar eclipse in other [accounts], these men ascribe it to the same natural cycle, bolstered by the testimony of astronomers, who say that the fluids within all things are moved by a certain force and potency of the moon. Fear forced [people] to side with various opinions. And whatever damages they could not escape by foresight, they dismissed through disputation.

The water had already risen immensely, and it was not the place for disputations, since they saw before their eyes the debris of their neighbors' houses turning over and over [in the floodwaters]. Even more distressing for those fearing and watching these things was that all ways of escape were already blocked. Only starvation was left as consolation for being alive. Fear had so invaded the improvident and wretched hearts of mortals that people seemed out of their minds and speechless. The less they spoke, the more the silence seemed terrifying and threatening. For they imagined that those who were not speaking had been killed by starvation or by the waters. Only groans and laments were heard from those who could speak. In sum, everything was full of grief and very sad to see.

The Tiber had begun to offer a sign of this flooding before noon. As the waters increased, all the low-lying parts of the city and underground places gradually filled. Nor were the waters seen above ground before they first made their way in through underground channels. [D2v] For the low-lying areas and underground cellars of many spots had been filled with water, though the waters did not reach the ground level of those buildings. But after all the low-lying areas of the city had been filled with water, as if by treachery and stealth, the Tiber began to wander at will through the city's streets

---

Website, "Five Millennium Catalog of Solar Eclipses" at https://eclipse.gsfc.nasa.gov/SEcat5/SE1501–1600.html; and "Five Millennium Catalog of Lunar Eclipses" at https://eclipse.gsfc.nasa.gov/LEcat5/LE1501–1600.html. The NASA website uses the Julian calendar, as is appropriate.

Fig. 9a. Flood marker for the 1530 flood located on the wall of the Caserma Giacomo Acqua just inside the Porta Flaminia in Piazza del Popolo. Photograph of December 2022 © Chiara Bariviera with kind permission.

and districts with greater force, as if it had intended to obliterate the city down to its foundations with water. [The waters] launched the first attack on the bridge of Hadrian, which is now called Sant'Angelo. It was there that Father Tiber wished to take back those

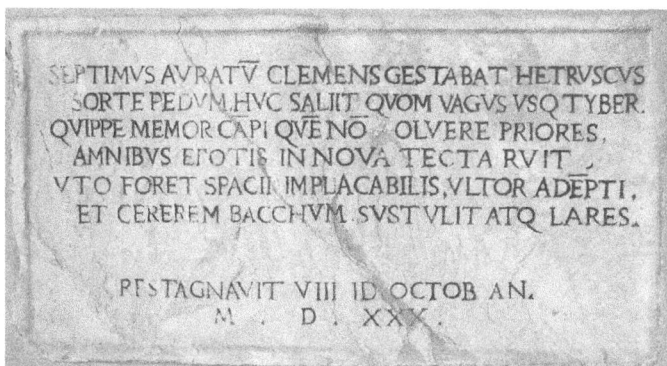

SEPTIMVS AVRATV CLEMENS GESTABAT HETRVSCVS
SORTE PEDVM.HVC SALIIT QVOM VAGVS VSQ TYBER.
QVIPPE MEMOR CAPI QVE NO OLVERE PRIORES,
AMNIBVS ErOTIS IN NOVA TECTA RVIT
VTO FORET SPACII IMPLACABILIS,VLTOR ADEPTI,
ET CERErEM BACCHVM SVST VLIT ATQ LARES.

PFSTAGNAVIT VIII ID OCTOB AN.
M . D . XXX .

Fig. 9b. Detail of Fig. 9a, bottom inscription. © Chiara Bariviera with kind permission.

two arches of the ancient riverbed's bridge that had been closed off
to him by the building of the citadel [i.e., Castel Sant'Angelo, Fig.
10]. So, collecting water from all sides, he surrounded the citadel
and, making tunnels, tried to destroy it.[148] But after he had made
no progress, aroused by great fury, he called to his aid all the rivers,
springs, and streams.

It was already night when almost fifty rivers, led by Father Tiber,
came together to lay siege to the bridge and citadel. Many torrents
and swift streams also joined the allied battle lines of water.[149] After
the vortices and whirlpools of water were given their marching
orders, the Tiber attacked Hadrian's bridge again with a great roar,
such a great mass of water, so much power, and such a great mass
of violent whirlpools that you would think it the raging ocean. Thus,
he surrounded the bridge and covered it with water. Then, after
overturning its ledges and walls, with large and deep whirlpools he

---

148. Gómez seems to be referring to the two arches of the Ponte
Sant'Angelo, which were on land at the entrance of the Castel Sant'Angelo.
See Fig. 10 by Piranesi, which shows these two arches as they existed in the
seventeenth century. This area was significantly modified during the Tiber
embankment-wall construction in the 1880s. Gómez is saying that the
river wanted to resume its ancient course under these two arches. See also
Taylor, "Tiber River Bridges," 4–5. Gómez here uses the historical present to
intensify the sense of action; we have used the past tense.

149. Gómez here refers to the almost fifty tributaries of the Tiber.

Fig. 10. View of Ponte Sant'Angelo and Castel Sant'Angelo. Giovanni Battista Piranesi, "Veduta del Ponte e Castello Sant'Angelo," in Vedute di Roma. *Etching, 1754. The arches of the Ponte Sant'Angelo that are on land can be seen at the right (towards the Castello) in this eighteenth-century etching and would have also been visible to Gómez two centuries earlier.*

destroyed an entire section of the buildings that faced the money changers at the foot of the bridge. On the other side, [the river] lifted the foundations of the bridge in the region of the city across the Tiber, which provides the route from the citadel of Sant'Angelo to the [Apostolic] Palace.[150] He thought that he would destroy Hadrian's bridge in short order once those supports that strengthened it on both sides were removed. But the waters struggled in vain for a long time and could not defeat those structures, which had been founded on high piers and constructed on very firm bases. The Tiber, as if filled with shame, therefore attacked the street that is called Giulia with the great rush of his assembled waters.[151]

---

150. The name *Pons Transtyberinus* probably refers to the part of the Passetto di Borgo that crosses over the moat surrounding Castel Sant'Angelo. The Passetto di Borgo is an elevated passage built in 1277 by Pope Nicholas III (1277–80) that links the castle to the Vatican Palace.

151. Via Giulia was created by Pope Julius II (r.1503–13) in 1508 as a long, straight street on the left bank of the Tiber that he envisioned as a new urban administrative, judicial, and banking center. It was paralleled

This place once was its riverbed, its width extending to the tower that today is called Sabellica,[152] as some inscriptions discovered there now show. [The river] had been gradually expelled from there through the work of the common folk or plebeians and confined to narrow channels in the banks. Even though it tried over the years to win back the site of this lost riverbed with many floods, nevertheless it was never able to take possession, so difficult did it seem to shift such provident and well-fortified embankments. Therefore, after this business had been feigned and drawn out for many years, although everything was now safe and sound (and long lulled to sleep by forgetfulness), [the Tiber] plotted to avenge the injury to his occupied riverbed. In addition to the river and the torrents that he had previously drawn to his aid, he also called on the sun and the moon, allied deities of the heavens who during the eclipse [D3r] inflicted an increase of water.

Aided by such and so many auxiliaries, raging Tiber attacked the via Giulia now here, now there, shaking every building to its foundations. With a foaming mound of water, he dragged the structures opposing him into a whirlpool. Already the lofty and beautiful palace of Giuliano Ceci had fallen with a great roar and

---

by via della Lungara on the right bank. It is still a notable street in Rome lined with elegant palaces and churches, many of which, however, were constructed after 1530. See Maurizia Cicconi, "E il papa cambiò strada: Giulio II e Roma. Un nuovo documento sulla fondazione di via Giulia," *Römisches Jahrbuch der Bibliotheca Hertziana* 41 (2013/14): 227–59; Luigi Salerno, Luigi Spezzaferro, and Manfredo Tafuri, *Via Giulia: Una utopia urbanistica del 500* (Rome: Aristide Staderini, 1973); and Nicholas Temple, Renovatio Urbis: *Architecture, Urbanism and Ceremony in the Rome of Julius II* (London: Routledge, 2011), 34–93.

152. I.e., the Corte Savella, a courthouse controlled by the Savelli family, situated on via di Monserrato, near via Giulia. See Niccolò Del Re, *La Curia Capitolina e tre altri organi giudiziari romani* (Rome: Fondazione Marco Besso, 1993), 103–29; Irene Fosi, *Papal Justice: Subjects and Courts in the Papal State, 1500–1750,* Thomas V. Cohen, trans. (Washington, DC: Catholic University Press, 2011), 31–32; and Salerno, Spezzaferro, and Tafuri, *Via Giulia,* 128–29.

was ruined to its deepest foundations.[153] On the other side of the riverbank, those remarkable dining rooms of kings, constructed through the great and lofty efforts of Agostino Chigi and adorned with columns and lustrous with gold and multi-colored marbles, were covered by the waves. A good part of the garden was also torn apart by the whirlpools [Fig. 11].[154]

---

153. Giuliano Ceci (dates unknown) was a cleric and canon of San Giovanni in Laterano. He was a friend of Pomponio Leto (1428–98) and participated in Leto's humanist academy. See Wouter Bracke, *Fare la epistola nella Roma del Quattrocento* (Rome: Roma nel Rinascimento, 1992), 121–23. Ceci began construction on his palace in 1515. For the palace, which was the precursor of the famous Palazzo Falconieri designed by the architect Borromini, see Christoph Luitpold Frommel, "Il palazzo di Giuliano Ceci, precursore di Palazzo Falconieri," in *Il Palazzo Falconieri e il palazzo barocco a Roma: Atti del Convegno indetto all'Accademia d'Ungheria in Roma, Rome 24–26 maggio 1995*, Gábor Hajnóczi and Csorba László, ed. (Soveria Mannelli-Catanzaro: Rubbettino, 2009), 15–27; and Mary De Cubellis, "Palazzo Falconieri a via Giulia: Contributi alla conoscenza della fortuna dell'edilizia privata di Francesco Borromini" (MA diss., Università degli Studi di Roma "Tor Vergata," 2015/2016), neither of whom, however, mentions the 1530 collapse reported by Gómez. The census of 1527 lists Ceci living in Rione Regola, where most of via Giulia is located, as "Iuliano Chechio" in a household of eighteen. See Lee, *Habitatores in Urbe*, 234 (no. 5627). Ceci's graffito is present in the Catacombs of Priscilla in Rome, along with those of other academy members. See Richard J. Palermino, "The Roman Academy, the Catacombs and the Conspiracy of 1468," *Archivium Historiae Pontificiae* 18 (1980): 117–55, at 147. For the academy, see Ingrid D. Rowland, *The Culture of the High Renaissance: Ancients and Moderns in Sixteenth-Century Rome* (Cambridge: Cambridge University Press, 1998), 10–17. For Pomponio Leto, with extensive further bibliography, see "Repertorium Pomponianum," https://www.repertoriumpomponianum.it/; and Chiara Cassiani and Myriam Chiabò, ed., *Pomponio Leto e la prima accademia romana* (Rome: Roma nel Rinascimento, 2007).

154. Located on the via della Lungara and now known as the Villa Farnesina (after its later owners, the Farnese), this structure was built by Agostino Chigi (1466–1520). The villa, constructed between 1505 and 1510, was designed by Baldassarre Peruzzi, frescoed by Raphael among others, and included a beautiful garden that went down to the Tiber. Chigi

Fig. 11. View of the flooded church of Sto. Spirito in Sassia. From the Hall of Perspectives at the Villa Farnesina. Fresco by Baldassare Peruzzi, 1518–19.

69

But among the many other ruined dwellings, which I shall omit so as not to be long-winded, I must not pass over in silence the destruction of the studious and virtuous man Eusebio. Foretold by the ruin of others and presaged by the collapse of neighboring structures, this could not be avoided. For the Tiber, inflamed with fury, struck this man's house with a great rush of water and undermined it. Once its raging whirlpools tore it apart, the river dragged [the house] into the abyss. It also swallowed the man with his whole family and furniture in the whirlpools, so that hardly a trace of the building remained to be seen.[155] Wondrous to say, so great was the impetus of the water, so great the furor, that it overturned many buildings on via Giulia. Once considered a famous and illustrious street of the city, but now torn apart by the Tiber's pounding, it has become so infamous and so deformed by building debris that it is now abandoned by its own

---

was a wealthy banker from Siena who moved to Rome in 1486. He financed many papal projects and became a patron of the arts. See Rowland, *Culture*, 181–82. For the importance of urban gardens at that time, see David R. Coffin, *Gardens and Gardening in Papal Rome* (Princeton, NJ: Princeton University Press, 1991), 126–38; and Denis Riboullault, *Rome en ses jardins: Paysage et pouvoir au XVIe siècle* (Paris: CTHS/INHA, 2013), 259–62.

155. The catastrophe of this Eusebio is mentioned in other accounts of the 1530 flood. In a letter to Alessandro de' Medici (1510–37), the humanist Giovanni Battista Sanga (1496–1532) describes Eusebio as a man who was "once secretary to Cardinal San Giorgio." He reports that he was in his house with perhaps thirty other people when it collapsed, killing all the people and animals inside. The letter is reproduced by Carcani, *Il Tevere*, 45–46. See Appendix C below, pp, 133–35. Another account appears in an anonymous tract on the 1530 flood published in Bologna, which reports that Eusebio was master of the house of Cardinal San Giorgio, that Eusebio's own house cost 10,000 ducats, and that forty members of his "family" died with him. Appendix A below, pp, 124–32. "Family" in this context refers to servants and other household members as well as blood relatives. See Benvenuto Gasparoni, ed., *"Diluvio di Roma che fu a VII d'ottobre l'anno MDXXX [...]": Opusculo Pubblicato in Bologna nel 1530* (Rome: Tipografia delle Scienze Matematiche e Fisiche, 1865). This may be the same Eusebio who is listed in Rione Regola in the November 1527 census as "Eusebio escutero apostolico" (Eusebio apostolic examiner) with five members in his household. See Lee, *Habitatores in Urbe*, 234 (no. 5619).

residents and deserted. So indeed does fortune alter circumstances. Who would not rightly tremble, who would not be horrified on seeing the large and solid foundations of buildings on both sides of that street pierced, eroded, and overturned by waterways hidden underground? There was not a house there that had not collapsed or was showing signs of falling. How wretched the condition of mortals! How vain our plans! How changing and variable is hope in human affairs! How transient and fleeting our trust in them! How many and bitter their outcomes!

Earlier that morning, Rome had been safe enough and — since things were gradually getting better — happy and prosperous.[156] Then suddenly, in the space of a moment, everything was turned into grief and took on the appearance of pale death. Indeed — to say nothing of the old, boys and trembling girls — even the faces of robust youths grew so pale that they did not look like themselves. Caught unaware, they were imprisoned in their houses, tortured with fear and hunger. What seemed even more bitter, all escape routes had already been closed off by the water. What siege of enemy barbarians, what captivity, and finally, what sack could compare to this? In comparison, that captivity was the greatest freedom. For, while those captives enjoyed the free and serene sky, these were deprived of the enjoyment of all the elements and were shut in their houses amid these very elements, [D3v] and they died the death of Tantalus without glory.[157]

There was also no wine. Cruel Tiber had poured it into the waves. Nor was there any fuel for fire so that they might at least restore their wretched and afflicted bodies, which were colder than marble itself. But what shall I say about the water? Contaminated by putrefaction and corruption, it was impossible to drink without dying. Again, they had no supply of grain. Because [their reserves] were used up in previous calamities, they were living hand to mouth. In sum, at

---

156. I.e., gradually recovering from the terrible sack of 1527.

157. The mythical figure of Tantalus, son of Zeus, was a Lydian king. For abusing the privileges of the gods, he was made to stand in water that receded when he tried to drink. See Simon Hornblower, Anthony Spawforth, and Esther Eidinow, ed. *The Oxford Classical Dictionary*, 4th ed. (Oxford: Oxford University Press, 2012), 1430 s.v.

that moment more than ever were those verses of the divine [Virgil] Maro on tormented Troy appropriate for Rome, which was full of great lamentation:

Who could describe with words the disaster
Of that night, or who could give tears equal
To the pain? The ancient city falls....[158]

But what troubled people's minds more was the separation from beloved spouses and children, which happened to many by happenstance. As it happened, many had ventured outside their homes. Surrounded by the quickly rising waters, they were unable to return. It was impossible to learn from another's report whether people were alive, and what one easily imagined about another, he feared about himself. Adding to the fear was the earthquake that some felt just before the flood and that many reported afterward. At the same time, what some others were saying was also troubling their minds: that the sea was refusing to receive that influx of water but was blocking it with sand bars and wind.

So, they lived in hunger and fear, until the Tiber itself pulled back two days later and gave hope of breathing [again]. Yet the receding and decrease of the waters gave the city no less trouble than their rise had [given] it work and damage. For, [the river] had left us the city's dwellings in a weakened state. They were almost threatening to collapse. Frightening in their great squalor, they were filled with excrement and mud. To clean them up and stabilize them with rods and beams we could use only what our poor condition had left us. And there are the certainties after a flood: the high price of food and signs of disease, as well as a great fear and worry about the evil to come.

Some [astronomers], distorting [predictions] about changes of kingdoms and provinces, said that the influence that had been calculated for 1524 had been shifted to this [year], since the flood occurred during a lunar eclipse and under a clear sky and without many prior downpours. They proved it by this reasoning: that in many places the rivers and lakes increased.[159] The Po, during the

---

158. Verg. A. 2.360–61.

159. Along with Jakob Phlaun of Ulm, the astronomer Johannes Stöffler (1452–1531) published in *Almanach nova plurimis annis venturis inserentia*

same period, flooded the fields and brought great damage.[160] The Timavo also offered a sign when it overflowed its banks.[161] The ocean, too, produced unusual and terrible high tides, which reached Holland in the following month.[162] During these [high tides], the waves are remembered to have carried away many cities along with their inhabitants and to have destroyed the labors of men and beasts most tragically. Indeed, the pope [i.e., Clement VII] truly grieved

(1499) a prediction that a deluge would cover the world on February 20, 1524. His calculations foretold twenty planetary conjunctions during this year, sixteen of which would take place under the watery sign of Pisces. More than a hundred pamphlets were published endorsing this prophecy, which brought about widespread panic as the date approached. See Ottavia Niccoli, "Il diluvio del 1524 fra panico collettivo e irrisione carnevalesca," in *Scienze, credenze occulte, livelli di cultura: Convegno Internazionale di Studi (Firenze, 26–30 giugno 1980)* (Florence: L.S. Olschki, 1982), 369–92. See also Morten Steen Hansen, "Rainbow and the Incarnation: Lotto, Correggio, and the Deluge of 1524," in *Lorenzo Lotto: Contesti, significati, conservazione*, Francesca Coltrinari and Enrico Maria Dal Pozzolo, ed. (Ponzano Veneto: ZeL Edizioni, 2019), 206–25. Transformations in kingdoms and provinces refers to the astrological theory that linked the overturning of political regimes and epochs to planetary conjunctions. See Anthony Grafton, *Cardano's Cosmos: The Worlds and Works of a Renaissance Astrologer* (Cambridge, MA: Harvard University Press, 1999), 53–55; and Craig Martin, *Renaissance Meteorology: Pomponazzi to Descartes* (Baltimore: Johns Hopkins University Press, 2011), 71–73. We thank Craig Martin for advice on this section.

160. The Po River, which like the Tiber was prone to flooding, flows eastward across northern Italy and into the Adriatic Sea. For its management, see Franco Cazzola, "Le bonifiche cinquecentesche nella valle del Po: Governare le acque, creare nuove terre," in *Arte e scienza delle acque nel Rinascimento*, Alessandra Fiocca, Daniela Lamberini, and Cesare Maffioli, ed. (Venice: Marsilio, 2004): 15–35.

161. The Timavo River is a two-kilometer stream in the province of Trieste in northeast Italy. See Robert Macfarlane, *Underland: A Deep Time Journey* (New York: W.W. Norton 2020), 175–210.

162. Gómez here refers to St. Felix's Flood (November 8, 1530). On this flood and local memory of it, see Raingard Esser, "'Ofter gheen water op en hadde gheweest': Narratives of Resilience on the Dutch Coast in the Seventeenth Century," *Dutch Crossing* 40 (2016): 97–107.

about [D4r] these bad things and tried to remedy them in every respect with careful solutions. But since everything had been wiped out and devastated by the unfavorable conditions of the immediate past,[163] and because of the severe damage caused by the Tiber, the pious and very merciful prince was not able to carry out fully what he had planned, even though he had placed men in charge of this matter who would take care that not many citizens would suffer harm, and even though he had arranged many things in secret.[164]

SECTION 3: THE CONSEQUENCES OF FLOODS

It is arduous and unequal to my strength to describe the sequence of floods and their prodigious results with some brief reference to learned studies. For if we touch on the effects rather than on the causes of the events, this work will be pointless, being more onerous than praiseworthy. If, however, we discuss the origins of the events and what they necessarily forecast, this text will be worth reading and somewhat agreeable to the intellect. Yet it is [also] rather risky, since this is a matter that — in addition to an immense library of books — demands experience of natural events, which in my case is very little and as insignificant as is my ingenuity. Nevertheless, it will

---

163. I.e., the Sack of 1527.

164. See Kenneth M. Setton, *The Papacy and the Levant, 1204–1571*, 4 vols. (Philadelphia: American Philosophical Society, 1976–84), 3:553, who paraphrased a contemporary letter sent to the duke of Mantua that contained a vivid description of the catastrophe and its effect on Clement. The letter was transcribed by Marino Sanuto, *I Diarii di Marino Sanuto*, Guglielmo Berechet, Nicolò Barozzi, and Marco Allegri, ed. (Venice: Fratelli Visentini, 1899), 54, cols. 74–76. See Appendix E, pp. 140–42. It reports that returning from Ostia the pope entered Rome but, not able to reach the Vatican, was forced to spend two days in the church of Sant'Agata dei Goti near the Quirinal Hill. When finally returning to the Vatican, he saw the enormous ruin, which was followed by great food scarcity due to the destruction of the flour mills in the Tiber. See also Esposito, "Roma e i suoi diluvi," 24–25, for the procession that Clement organized to placate divine displeasure; and Giorgio Simoncini, *Roma: Le trasformazioni urbane nel Cinquecento I: Topografia e urbanistica da Giulio II a Clemente VIII* (Florence: L.S. Olschki, 2008), 89, 91. We thank Kenneth Gouwens for pointing out the Setton reference.

be somewhat useful that I have considered posterity and left them the beginnings of a rough [account] of the past. But lest this treatise grow too long, I turn to the subject itself.

Among ancient and more recent [writers], there has clearly been great and complex uncertainty concerning the occurrence of floods and what the outpouring of these waters portended. For the difficulty arises that none of those that I have examined explain the causes of the floods, even though historians have described many of their effects. Therefore, it will be worthwhile to investigate this comprehensively[165] so that what has not been treated so far can be briefly summarized. Among the other kinds of harm that floods bring us, they especially portend three evils, two of which happen accidentally. The third happens necessarily by a certain influx and by the very nature of floodwaters.[166]

Ruin and Destruction of Things from Floods
The first kind of damage is the destruction of buildings, the death of humans and animals, and the uprooting of trees. The waters bring this to us by accident and not by their specific nature since this harm can be avoided with human understanding and foreknowledge. This harm will be avoided if [D4v] we first investigate the power and nature of rivers. Once we have understood this, it will be useful to divert the force of these rivers by channels, to weaken it with outlets, and to contain it with embankments, piles, weirs, or wooden structures. For instance, Trajan ordered multiple channels to be dug in various places, as Pliny the Younger records in more than one place in book 10 of the *Epistles*.[167] Compelled by a similar concern, Caesar also built many canals at Lleida with which he could divert part of the

---

165. In the Latin edition, the verb appears as *perscutari*, a misprint. We read instead *perscrutari* "to be investigated thoroughly."

166. Gómez is making the Aristotelian distinction between accidental qualities and substantial form. The latter is essential and therefore necessary and universally true. See Arist. *Categories* 4a.17–20. On this distinction, see Teresa Robertson Ishii and Philip Atkins, "Essential vs. Accidental Properties," *Stanford Encyclopedia of Philosophy*, at https://plato.stanford.edu/entries/essential-accidental.

167. Plin. *Ep.* 10. 41–42, 61–62.

Segre River.[168] Semiramis, in order to limit floods caused by the overflowing Euphrates, covered the embankments with asphalt four cubits thick because she was not satisfied with bricks alone.[169] Cyrus, king of the Persians, so divided the Gyndes River by digging multiple canals that he reduced it to such a minimal depth that, according to Herodotus, it could be crossed with practically dry feet.[170] Near the tomb of Alyattes in Sardis, an artificial lake was created to capture floodwaters.[171] Myris dug a lake near Memphis, as Herodotus attests, so that it would capture the [waters of the] Nile when they raged more violently.[172] We read that the same was done with regard to the Euphrates. For among the Mesopotamians Nitocris slowed the Euphrates, when it was flowing too fast, with curved and winding channels, as the same author writes.[173] While sailing the Nile,

---

168. Lleida (Lérida) is a Spanish city in the Catalonia region and is on the right bank of the river Segre. In 49 BCE, during the Civil War, it was besieged by Caesar, who defeated L. Afranius and M. Petreius, legates of Pompey the Great (Caes. *Civ.* 1. 29–47). On this occasion, Caesar decided to dig some channels along the river to divert its course and create an artificial ford. In this way, he made it possible for his army to cross the river and chase his enemies (Caes. *Civ.* 1.62).

169. Semiramis, mythical Assyrian queen and founder of Babylonia (r.1356–1314 BCE), built a tunnel under the Euphrates to connect her palaces on the opposite sides of the river. To do so, she temporarily diverted the course of the river into an artificial pond. Then, she built a vaulted tunnel, the walls of which had a brick facade covered with asphalt, before letting the waters of the river return to its bed (Diod. Sic. 2.1). Asphalt is a naturally occurring petroleum-like material used in antiquity as caulk or sealant for reservoirs and other water-bearing structures.

170. Hdt. 1.189.

171. Hdt. 1.193. Alyattes was the father of Croesus, and his grave mound is in Bin Tepe (Tukey), the necropolis of Sardis, capital of Lydia.

172. Hdt. 2.101.

173. According to Herodotus, to protect the city from the Medes, Queen Nitocris of Babylon altered the course of the Euphrates, built a monumental embankment along both of its banks, and created an artificial basin (Hdt. 1.185).

Ptolemy also opened a canal to control the force of the river. After sailing through it, he closed it [again], according to Diodorus.[174]

In addition to these [measures], care of the riverbed and removal of rubble and materials that have fallen into the river are [necessary], so that [the riverbed] provides the waters an easy way out. If these things are neglected, it easily happens that tree branches pile up and sand and stones increase day by day. The riverbed therefore grows shallower and [the river] may overturn structures with its aggressive whirlpools and the violence of its crashing waves. Also, it may sometimes diverge completely, abandoning its former and older riverbed and turning elsewhere, just as the Meander and the Euphrates often did.

Here we are not demanding those magnificent and sumptuous embankments of the ancient Romans (about which we spoke in more detail in book 1). Rather, it will be enough to repel the force of the water, [to build] a dike made out of bundles of branches and leafy bushes cut from the fields, or from the rubble of ruined buildings, or even from piles of tree trunks and stones interwoven or held together with hardened mud (as Nitocris did among the Assyrians), like bundles of herbs for drying, such as we see control the largest rivers in Gaul.[175] Yet, if we want to turn part of the river elsewhere or divert it into channels or lakes, we should be careful lest embankments be built against the current or in some way across it before we have considered the depth and height of both places.

For we shall not lament happening to us what happened to King Artanater.[176] Either because he did not know how rivers worked or, as it is believed, out of a desire to spread his name, he obstructed the Melas River, which flowed into the Euphrates, by constructing embankments at its exit. Therefore, he made it slow and swollen, so that it flooded the entire region. [Er] Not long after, battered by the waters, that massive embankment broke apart with so many whirlpools and so much force that it took many fields with it and devastated a large part of Galatia and Phrygia. The Senate sentenced

---

174. Diod. Sic. 1.33.1.

175. Alberti, *On the Art of Building*, 348 (10.11); and Alberti, *L'architettura* [*De re aedificatoria*], 2:954–55 (10.11).

176. I.e., Ariarathes (V?), king of Cappadocia (Strabo 12.2.8).

the man to pay thirty talents. The same thing would have happened to Iphicrates. While besieging Stymphalis, he tried to obstruct the water of the Erasinus River by throwing innumerable sponges in it. Yet he desisted after he recalled Jupiter's admonition.[177] Therefore, when diligent and precise care has been applied, this first trouble from floods can be easily foreseen and made good.

HUNGER

The second evil of flooding is hunger and the high cost of everything. This also happens by chance and only by flooding that occurs before the harvest is gathered. If it happens after grain is laid up in storehouses, the flood does not bring any damage to those who have had foresight. If it does bring [damage], it is such that the famine can be easily relieved by grain from neighboring provinces. Therefore, where harm can be removed or born more easily through human planning and foresight, we shall judge it to have happened by accident.[178]

PESTILENCE

By its very nature, the third and irreparable injury that floods portend to us is pestilence. This cannot be addressed by any human skill or ingenuity unless God has been appeased. Although it can originate from multiple causes, which Giovanni di San Nazaro explains more fully in the book *On Pestilence*, it is clear that it arises especially from stagnant water mixed with mud, as Galen demonstrates in the book *On the Differences of Fevers*.[179] This mud, when activated with

---

177. On Iphicrates and his sponges, see Strabo 8.8.4.

178. Referring again to the distinction between essential and accidental properties (see above p. 75 n. 166). Gómez argues that if human planning can mitigate the effects of flooding, then flooding is "accidental," i.e., neither necessary nor essential. Human planning cannot alter the nature of things, however, and so he is trying to sort out the effects that must necessarily occur from those that happen only due to a lack of wise planning and therefore could be prevented.

179. Also known as Gianfrancesco Riva di San Nazarro (1480–1535). See his *Tractatus de Peste* (Lyons: Jacques Saccon, 1522), *Quaestio* 5.

heat, emits some certain lethal and disease-bearing vapors.[180] These deprive human hearts of sense and affect them with a disease like the one that Thucydides records happened among the Athenians, and like the one that devastated almost all of Illyria in the same way, as Appian from Alexandria testifies.[181] Therefore, since floods bring a great amount of mud and filth from every place and drag many reptiles and corpses, it is certain that vapors must necessarily be created and emitted that afflict human bodies, as everyone knows occurred at the time of Pelagius.[182] And the savage pestilence that historians say occurred in Rome under Emperor Leo the Isaurian — when more than 300,000 people died of plague — as well as many others that we described in the second part, we must believe came from this same cause.[183]

This problem could therefore be generated more easily in Rome from the aforesaid cause: for in Rome cavities [Ev], underground waterways, sewers, and hidden spaces are abundant. The mud, when mixed with [flood]waters, [spreads] through them and cannot be completely removed or dried out over time. Rather, these places always remain humid, slimy, and dirty, and in certain areas filthy and full of excrement. When we inhale the air generated by the humidity emitted from these caves, it becomes condensed and rotten, thick, and dense through a certain condensation of exhalations and vapors. This air clings in a certain way to the forehead, and it presses and debilitates the eyes and gives off a deadly vapor. This is why, among other peoples, the Egyptians who look towards Libya in particular take pride in the

---

180. Gómez is referring to the theory of miasma: that bad air causes disease. See Jean-Pierre Leguay, *L'air et le vent au Moyen Âge* (Rennes: Presses Universitaires de Rennes, 2011), 67–99; and Renato Sansa, "L'odore del contagio: Ambiente urbano e prevenzione delle epidemie nella prima età moderna," *Medicina e Storia* 2 (2002): 83–108.

181. Thuc. 2.47–54; App. *Ill.* 3.1.4.

182. This refers to Pope Pelagius II who died in 590 after the flood of 589. See above, pp. 51–53.

183. Gómez refers here to Leo III the Isaurian (r.717–41). We have not been able to identify the plague mentioned here as occurring in this time, and consequently we have been unable to identify the historians to which Gómez refers.

fact that their air is never corrupted or changed by vapors, and that they therefore are in excellent health, as Herodotus reports.[184]

I think, in fact, that this happens through motion: vapors rising from the ground either dissipate or they are thoroughly cooked by heat-inducing motions. For air becomes better with motion. Just as water goes bad when it does not move, so too, when it is enclosed, air deteriorates and gives very unfortunate results, as Antonio Guainerio testifies in his treatise *Pestilence*, chap. 1. There he reports that he had learned these things about water [stored] on certain ships. [Another example comes from] above the countryside of the Ticino in the fortified town of Nicolino Beccaria, where the enclosed poisonous air poured out and killed those who opened a well.[185] In addition, [Julius] Capitolinus the historian reports that in Babylonia, in the temple of Apollo, a very ancient golden small box was found, in which there was enclosed corrupted and equally poisonous air. When the small box was broken open, this air spread out and not only killed those who were then nearby but also brought a terrible plague, [which spread] by contagion throughout Asia all the way to Parthia.[186] We read in the historian Ammianus Marcellinus that at the time of Marcus [Aurelius] Antoninus and Lucius Verus a temple in Seleucia was destroyed and the statue of Apollo Comeo was brought to Rome. [Driven by] the desire for spoils, the soldiers found a narrow opening previously closed by the Chaldean priests. As soon as they opened it, such an atrocious and disgusting pestilential vapor burst out that everything was infected with a horrible and deadly disease from the boundaries of Persia all the way to Gaul.[187]

---

184. Hdt. 2. 25–26.

185. The Ticino River originates in Switzerland and enters the Po River near Pavia. Antonio Guainerio (c.1412–c.1445), *De peste* (Venice: Rinaldo da Nimega, 1440), 1, fol. 3v., speaks of vapors rising from the bilges of a ship and infecting the sailors. Guainerio, a Pavian, also recounts the story of people killed by the gases released when they opened a well.

186. SHA *Verus* 8.

187. Amm. Marc. 23.6.24. On Ammianus' possible motives for discussing this case, see R.L. Rike, Apex Omnium: *Religion in the* Res Gestae *of Ammianus* (Berkeley: University of California Press, 1987), 27–28.

From what has been said, it is clear that air permeated by vapor inflicts just as much damage as the mud from floods, since [the mud] gives rise to that humid air, as Servius also reports about a dried-out swamp, which produced pestilence.[188] The Nile also produced a severe plague after it rose higher than usual and left many different animals encased in mud, which putrified as they dried out. Rome, too, which was once excessively shaded by its porticoes and eaves, was also unhealthy in the summer, as Pomponio [Leto] and [Flavio] Biondo record, simply [E2r] because the vapors of the earth and the Tiber mist were enclosed in these very narrow porticoes.[189] For this reason, physicians resolved that it was conducive to the good health of the inhabitants neither to have overly narrow or obstructed streets, lest they trap thick, damp air, nor streets that were too wide, in order that they not be heated excessively by the sun. As Cornelius Tacitus writes, Nero had widened the streets of Rome, and [the city] was made less healthy because of this on account of the heat of the sun, which had made it hotter.[190]

Therefore, a happy medium should be maintained lest the streets be so wide as to eliminate shade or so narrow that the air putrifies, as easily happens in Rome. In his book, *On the Site of Ancient Rome,* Pier [Paolo] Vergerio testifies that those "cities either destroyed by a violent event or consumed by age have unhealthy air," since many cavities and subterranean places are blocked by ruins and [therefore]

---

188. Servius' reference is to the swamp of Atina in the Pontine Marshes, south of Rome (Serv. *A.* 7.630).

189. We thus far have been unable to locate this reference in the writings of either Biondo or Pomponio. Porticoes that extended into the streets, encumbering street traffic, were considered a problem in fifteenth- and early sixteenth-century Rome. For example, a statute issued by Nicholas V in 1452, governing the city officials known as the "masters of the streets" included a clause that forbade porticoes unless licensed by these city officials. For the statute, see Emilio Re, "Maestri di Strada," *Archivio della R. Società Romana di Storia Patria* 43 (1920), 86–102, clause 25. See also Long, *Engineering,* 45–46; and Anna Modigliani, *Roma al tempo di Leon Battista Alberti (1432–1472)* (Rome: Roma nel Rinascimento, 2019), 193–200.

190. Tac. *Ann.* 15.43. On how ancients designed the streets to prevent bad winds from affecting the air, see also Vitr. *De arch.* 1. 6.

emit foul air. In this category he puts Rome, Aquileia, Ravenna, Senigallia, Adria, and many other ancient cities that have suffered collapse through the ravages of time.[191]

Indeed, nothing harms human nature more than humid air. Physicians affirm that the south wind is more harmful than the other winds to human beings and animals. For they think that when the south wind blows, animals in pastures are in danger and that storks do not easily rely on south winds. Dolphins, too, hear sounds through the north wind, but when the south wind is blowing, they hear them with a delay and only if they are approaching [the sounds] head on. They also say that when the north wind blows, eels can remain without water for six days; but when the south wind blows, they cannot. [They say] that, because of its density and thickness, [the south wind] contains so much noxious power that they call it "life destroying."

They think that all living bodies waste away from humidity but recover with dryness and heat.[192] For that reason, Appian wrote on this subject that Numidians especially have a long life because they do not have winters.[193] Regardless of whether this kind of humid air is caused by the topography of the region, by the filth of sewers (which, as jurists say under the heading "On Sewers,"[194] makes the sky pestilential and threatens the ruin of buildings unless they are cleaned), or by the mud brought by the floodwaters, it therefore seems clear enough that this evil cannot be avoided by human planning but is due to a certain natural property of the thing itself.

Yet, what results from floodwaters is harsher. For, when mud mixed with water invades the subterranean places and hidden cavities

---

191. The four cities from Aquileia to Adria are positioned from north to south on the Adriatic coast of Italy. For the text, see Leonard Smith, "Pier Paolo Vergerio: *De Situ Veteris et Inclyte Urbis Rome," The English Historical Review* 41 (1926): 571–77, at 573.

192. Gómez has taken this discussion of the winds directly from Alberti, *On the Art of Building*, 11 (1.3). See also Alberti, *L'architettura* [*De re aedificatoria*], 1:30–31 (1.3). Alberti in turn is articulating ancient ideas about the salubrity of diverse winds, for example, Vitr. *De arch.* 1.4.1–8.

193. App. *Pun.* 10.71.

194. *Dig.* 43.23.

of a city, these cannot be cleaned. The air therefore becomes infected. Conduits and sewers confer great benefit on cities, however, if they can be skillfully cleaned and purged. For this reason, just as having well-cleaned conduits and sewers contributes to the good health of cities, so having dirty ones or not having any into which household waste — which makes the air denser — may be channeled and flow away, contribute to their unhealthiness. [E2v] Historians therefore say that the city of Smyrna, where Dolabella liberated Trebonius with a siege,[195] was the most beautiful among cities because of the design of its streets and decoration of its buildings. Otherwise it was filthy and unhealthy because there were no sewers that could receive the filth and waste it produced. For this reason, it displeased visitors with its stench. They say the same thing about the Etruscan city of Siena, which for the adornment and comfort of the city lacks only sewers. This is why the whole city not only stinks at the first and last vigils of the night,[196] when people pour chamber pots full of waste out of their windows; but it is also why it is dirty and very damp between these times. We ourselves have occasionally experienced this, just as Alberti writes in book 1 of *On Architecture*.[197]

It is therefore quite clear from all this how much damage and how much harm are brought by the sewage-laden mud that has been gathered and mixed with floodwaters from all over. As has often been said, this mud is spread through the blocked-up places of the city and closed within underground cavities, sewers, and passages. It then gives rise to pestilence out of a certain necessity, as it has often done and as we described in the second section of [this] treatise.

Since all these things are placed in God Almighty's hands and cannot be avoided through human planning, we piously ask Him that He consider it worthy to turn His hand to our purposes and in the end to have mercy on our great efforts.

195. Dio Cass. 42.29, 43.51, 44.22, 46.40, 47.30.

196. According to Roman timekeeping, the *prima vigilia* corresponded to the hours from 6:00 to 9:00 PM, the *ultima vigilia* (i.e., *quarta*) to the hours from 3:00 to 6:00 AM.

197. Alberti mentions the stench of Siena because of the dumping of chamber pots in *De re aedificatoria* 4.7. See Alberti, *On the Art of Building*, 113; and Alberti, *L'Architettura*, 1:324–25.

The End
At Rome at F. Minizio Calvo[198]
Year 1531
≈ ≈
≈

---

198. See p. 20 n. 8.

26

paſſa, & plura etiam ædificia aquarum violentia corruérunt . Sed
in plena & opulentiſſima vrbe / nequicquam talis alluuio quanti
nis maxima , mentes ciuium turbauerat . Auro enim vndique af
fluebat Roma , neque iam poterat tunc maguitudinem ſuam ſuſ
ſtinere . In tanto igitur diuitiarum exceſſu, in tam ampla rerum om
nium abundantia , conueniens alioqui & opportuna fuit alluuio , ſu
cuti infirmo ſanguine multo ac adipe repleto phlobotomia . Solent
enim plerunque proſperæ ac nimium ſecundæ res longe hominem a
ſe auocare : & cum ſeipſum non intelligat : rerum omnium Seruatoſ
rem negligat, atque contemnat. Bona igitur fuit alluuio , quæ ad ſe
hominem redire coegit , ac veluti ſtimulo aduerſitatis tactum , quæ
vera & iuſta ſunt agnoſcere . Habuerūt tamen inundationes iſtæ hoc
plus admirationis , quod parum euidenti cauſa ſubita illa inundatio
corigerit / quū ne pluuio quidem cœlo vt quidam aiebant , flumina
ercuiſſent : & qued dierum interuallo non vno ſit die ea clades euaſ
gata . Scio enim non defuiſſe : qui fingerent molem iſtam aquaſ
rum ex imbribus alpium proueniſſe , decuſſaque vi ventorum arſ
borum folia cauſam præſtitiſſe , vt torrentes multi vno impeſ
tu in ſubiecta flumina præcipitati, inſuetum fecerint incrementum.
Sed ſiue hæc fuit cauſa , ſiue alia magis occulta , inſueta rei facies in
prodigium verſa eſt . Multi ad tumultuoſum in Italiam Gallorū
deſcenſum , prodigium illud aquarum retulerunt , quo tempore &
Alphonſus iunior Neapolitano regno excidit : & Ferdinandus pater
medio belli apparatu fato obiit . Alii ad aliam cauſam referebant.
Nec deſunt , qui inundatione iſtam Tyberis in Vltimos Alexandri
annos conferant. Verum hoc parum negotii dabit , ſi tempora nu
merentur , quæ pluribus locis Romæ deſcripta leguntur . Nam in
lapide Tyburtino eccleſiæ Sancti Iacobi ſub anno a partu Virginis
M c c c e v c. Nonis decembris ſcribitur inundatio , quæ rela
ta ad tempora Alexandri , incidit in ſecundum eius Pontificatus an
num plus minus .

   Vigeſimatertia inundatio .
Eram ego maiori otio ſcripturus cladem iſtam miſerabilem tam mul
tis calamitatibus ſociatā,quā Tyberis inundatio intulit anno ſalutis.
M .   D .   X .   X .   X .
Sed creſcentibus indies curis/ & inter officia publica quotidianis aſ
ctionibus , quæ me vinctum penitus & occupatum tenent : futurum
erat : vt ſi hoc negocium in aliud tempus reiicerem : minus fortaſſis
haberem otii . Dum igitur récens tanti mali eſt memoria , dum

Sample page from Gómez, De prodigiosis Tyberis Inundationibus ab orbe condito ad
annum MDXXXI Commentarii. *Rome: Francesco Minizio Calvo, 1531, sig. Dv.*

animus adhuc in luctu est præsentis calamitatis, operæprecium duxi rem ipsam quamabsolutissime perstringere . Illuxerat nobis Saturni dies infanda, quæ octaua mensis numera tur Octobris : in qua Tyberis solito alueo dimotus, aquarum mon tes traduxit in Vrbem cum ingenti omnium admiratione & damno. videbantur enim vno illo die elementa omnia coniurasse . Fatiga bat dulces animas pauor ingens, ex ruentium ædificiorum crepitu. Percutiebat insuper miserorum pectora præteritorum malorum re cordatio : quorum adhuc recentes fuerant cicatrices . Iam alii ad vindictam scelerum immisisse Deum inundationem istam asserebant Indiciis quibusdam assertiones suas comprobantes : quod videlicet sereno cœlo , nec præcedentibus magnis imbribus irruperit tam ingens vis aquarum , quasi quod fontes abyssi dissolui viderentur. Addebant Eccly psin Solis & Lunæ : quæ eodem gradu , eodem etiam inundationis die contigerat . Alii vero istam naturali rerum cursui tribuebant . Simul etiam memorabát inundationem illam, quæ Benedicti . xii . tempore toto orbe naturaliter contigit, vt no uissimi quidam retulerunt , quando nullis præcedentibus imbri bus , terra sponte sua ruptis interioribus venis , ad modū diluuii sca turientium aquarum edidit torrentes : quibus prope infinita dam na mortalibus illata leguntur . Et iam Lunæ Ecclypsin in alios retorquentes ad eundem naturæ cursum referebát Astronomorum testimonio innixi , qui vi quadam & potentia Lunæ omnium rerum humorem dicunt commoueri . Sic igitur in varias ire sententias co gebat pauor,& quæ non poterant damna prouidendo tollere, alter eando solabantur . Iam aquæ in immensum creuerant, nec altere sationibus locus erat, cum ante oculos obuersarentur ruinæ vicino rum tectorum ,& quod acerbius fuerat : timentibus & cernentibus illas omnes fugiendi aditus præclusi erát . Sola inedia in consola tionem vitæ relicta. Vsqueadeo improuida & misera mortalium cor da inuaserat timor, vt homines amętes viderentur / & elingues, & quo minus loquebátur tanto magis suspectum & horribile videbatur silentium . Putabant enim non loquentes inedia aut aquis interem ptos . Nec eorum, qui loqui poterát , audiebantur nisi gemitus & lamętationes. In summa / omnia erát plena luctus & tristissimi aspe ctus. Inceperat inūdationis huius dare signū Tyberis ante meridie/ & crescéribus magis aquis carptim omnes vrbis concauitates & sub terranea loca implebant, nec prius super terram videbátur, q̄ sibi prius aditū per subterraneos meatus faceret, multoꝗ etenim inferiori

D ii

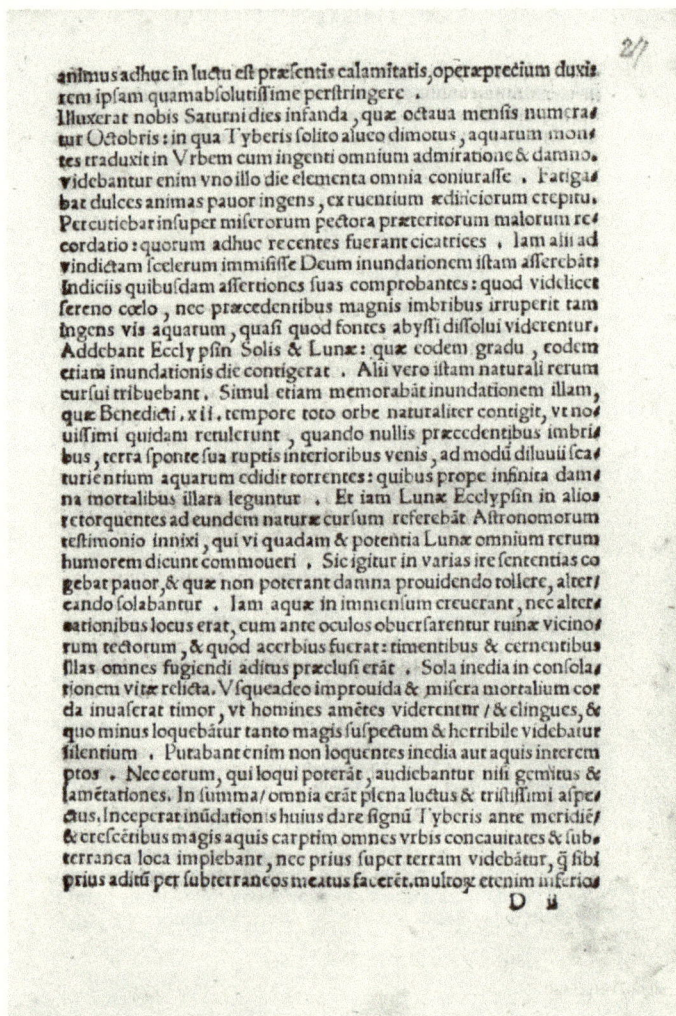

Sample page from Gómez, De prodigiosis Tyberis Inundationibus ab orbe condito ad annum MDXXXI Commentarii. *Rome: Francesco Minizio Calvo, 1531, sig. D2r.*

ſtes ſeu ſubterraneæ cellæ impletæ aquis fuerāt, ad quaſq; ædium ſu
perficiem aquæ minime peruenerūt. Poſtq; vero omnia vrbis cōcaua
quaſi per inſidias & clanculū repleta aquis fuerāt, maiori impetu eœ
vpit Tyberis per vias & regiones vrbis pro libito diuagari, & aquarū
torrētes immittere, quaſi quod vrbe a ſedibus imis, aquis obruere
deſtinaſſet. Et primū impetum fecerūt in pontem Adriani, qui nunc
dicitur. S. Angeli, vbi pater Tyberinus duos illos pontis arcus aluei
antiqui/qui ſibi ſub ædificio arcis precluſi fuerāt, reperere volēs col
lectis vndiq; aquis/ arcem circūdat: & factis cuniculis euertere tētat.
Sed cum nihil profeciſſet, magno veluti furore percitus, flumina om
nia/ fontes/ & amnes in auxilium vocat. Iam nox erat quādo ad obſi
dionem pōris & arcis quinquaginta fere flumina, quibus Tyberis pa
ter præerat ſe iſii addiderāt, pter torrētes plures & rapidiſſimos am
nes/ qui certatim ſocia aquaſq; agmina iungebāt . Tūc Tyberinus
inſtructis vorticibus, & aquæ turbinibus, Adriani pōtem iterū ma
gno murmure adoritur, tāto aquaſq; cumulo/ tāta vi/ tanta deniq; tur
binum eōgerie/ vt Oceanū ſæuiētem putares . Cingit itaq; pontem
ab omni latere, atq; aquis tegit, ac ſubuerſis eius ſubgrundiis & pa
rietibus/ totam illam ædificiorum partem, quæ ad radices pontis
Nummularios reſpicit, magnis & profundis voraginibus diſſipa
uit . Ab alia vero parte Pontem Tranſtyberinum, qui ab arce San
cti Angeli ad Palatium viam præſtat, a fundamentis ſuſtulit, id fu
turum ratus, vt pontem Adriani præſidiis, quibus hinc inde ſubni
xus erat, ſublatis/ paruo negotio euerteret . Sed cum incaſſum
diu aquæ certarent, neque machina illa altis fundata molibus, ac
firmiſſimis conſtructa baſibus expugnari poſſet, Tyberis veluti tur
bore ſuffuſus, collectis denique aquis, maiori impetu viam, quam
dicunt Iuliā, aggreditur. Hic locus olim alueus eius erat, cuius lati
tudo ad turrim, quam hodie appellant Sabellicam, protendebatur,
vt nunc ibi inuenti lapides monſtrant, a quo fuerat vulgi ſeu ple
beiorum manu paulatim eiectus, & ad anguſtiſſimas riparū fauces
redactus, quem quidem aluei amiſſi locum, licet olim inundatio
nibus pluribus recuperare tentaret, nuſquam tamen compos fieri
poterat, adeo difficile videbatur prouidos & munitos detentores
propellere . Simulato igitur & dilato in plures annos negocio,
cum iam omnia tuta & ſecura eſſent, ac longa obliuione ſopita,
deſtinat occupati aluei iniuriam vlciſci, & præter flumina & tor
rentes: quos prius in ſui auxilium traxerat : Solem etiam & Lu
nam conſcia numina Diuum inuocat : qui Eeclypſi præſentes ma

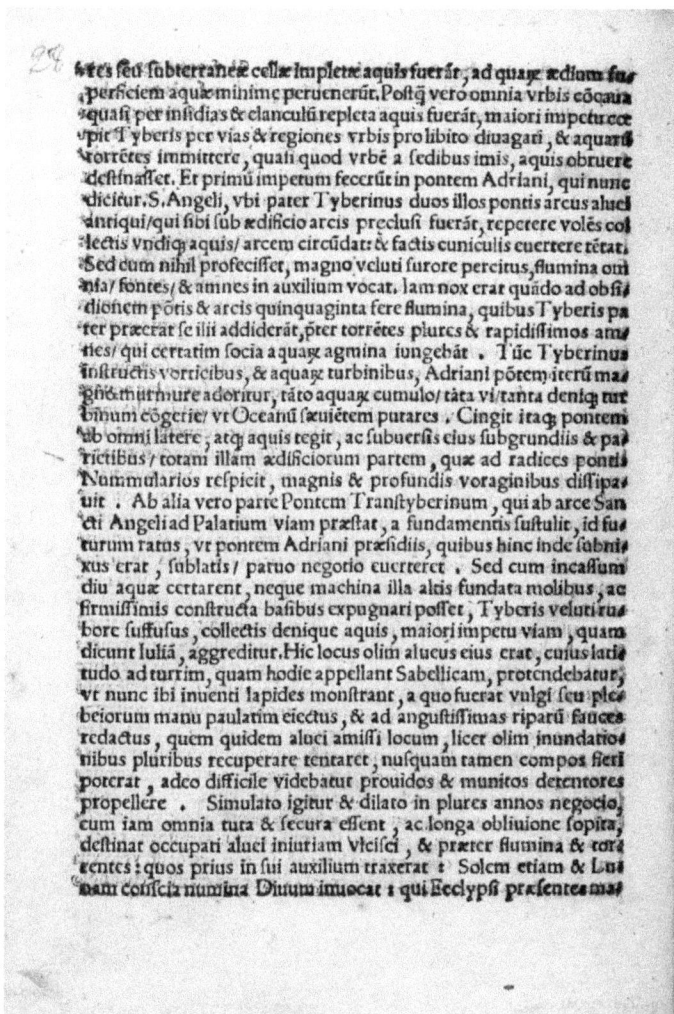

Sample page from Gómez, De prodigiosis Tyberis Inundationibus ab orbe condito ad annum MDXXXI Commentarii. *Rome: Francesco Minizio Calvo, 1531, sig. D2v.*

21

umnuni aquarum Incrementum intulerunt. Sic itaque tot & tan
tis præsidiis adiutus Tyberis viam Iuliā aggreditur furés modo hic,
modo illic: a fundamentis ædificia omnia cócutiens, spumosoq; aqua
rum cumulo oppositas trahebat gurgite moles. Iam domus præalta
& decora Iuliani Ceciimagno fragore lapsa a sedibus imis ruinā de
derat. Ab alio vero Ripæ latere ingentia illa Regū cœnacula Augu
stini Chisii præaltis/& magnis instructa molibus/ornata colūnis/auro
picturatisq; lapillis illustria cū bona viridarii parte vorticibus cōoul
sa tegebantur vndis. Sed inter plures alias tectoȝ ruinas, quas ne
fim prolixior, omittam, nō erit silentio innoluenda clades studiosi &
honesti viri Eusebii/ quæ veluti aliorum ruina densisesata, ac vicinaȝ
ædium prolapsionibus præmonita, non potuit cuitari. Huius enim
viri domum Tyberis furore accésus:tanto aquarum impetu cócussit:
ita suffoditæ: vorticibus furentibus reuulsam in abyssum traxit:ac
hominem cum supellectile & familia tota voraginibus absorbuit, vt
vix operis vestigia appareant:mirum dictu q; tantus fuerit hic aquaȝ
impetus,tantus furor:vt tot ædificia euerteret: adeo q; via Iulia inter
famosas & cóspicuas vi bis vias quōdā habita:nunc concussione Ty
beris dehiscens:ita sit effecta infamis:ita ædificioȝ ruinis deformata
vt a propriis eius inquilinis destituta/ sit iam deserta. Sic enim vat̄
at fortuna vices. Nam quis merito nō contremiscat? quis non hor
teat: cum viderit illius viæ tam magna ædificiorum:ac firma funda
menta:ab vtraq; parte locata occultis & subterraneis aquarū cunicu
lis perfossa:corrosa:atq; cōoulsa:& adeo concussa:vt nulla ibi sit do
mus: quæ nō fuerit lapsa: aut signum ruinæ dederit. O misera mor
talium cōditio/O inanes cogitatus nostri/q̃ fluxa/& varia est rerū hu
manarum spes:q̃ mutabilis & caduca illarum cōfidentia : quam varī
& acerbi illarum casus. Fuerat Roma matutino illo die satis secura:
& rebus paulatim prospere succedētibus/l̄.ilaris & læta : Cū ecce bre
ui temporis spatio versa sunt omnia in luctū & mutata in speciē pall̄
dæ mortis. Nam/vt senes ipsos:pueros: trepidasq; puellas omittam,
Pallebant adeo ora robustiorum Iuuenum vt propriā eorum faciem
non præ se ferrent. Detinebantur enim improuidi:domibus carce
rati:torquebantur timore & fame:& quod acerbius videbatur:omnes
fugiendi aditus aquis præclusi fuerant. Quæ vnquam Barbatorū
hostium obsidio: quæ captiuitas:quæ deniq; direptio huic poterit cō
parari: huius enim comparatione/ illorum captiuitas:summa erat li
bertas. Fruebantur enim captiui libero & sereno cœlo:isti vero vsu
omnium elementorum priuati:inter ipsa elementa clausi tectisq; inglo

Sample page from Gómez, De prodigiosis Tyberis Inundationibus ab orbe condito ad annum MDXXXI Commentarii. *Rome: Francesco Minizio Calvo, 1531, sig. D3r.*

TRANSCRIPTION OF THE LATIN TEXT

This transcription is based upon the only known text of Gómez's work on Tiber flooding. We have expanded Latin abbreviations and adapted capitalization, punctuation, and paragraphing to accord with modern usage. In transcribing "u" and "v" we have adopted the form that accords with modern orthography, i.e. "*uerbum*" > "*verbum*."

For accuracy of reference, the number-letter references in brackets throughout the translation and Latin refer to the signatures and foliation of the 1531 edition. We have included the pagination of the English translation in the margins of the Latin text.

※

DE PRODIGIOSIS TYBERIS INUNDATIONIBUS AB ORBE CONDITO   17
AD ANNUM MDXXXI COMMENTARII, REVERENDI D. LUDOVICI
COMESII, SACRI PALATII AUDITORIS AC VIRI UNDECUNQUE
DOCTISSIMI

[A2r] Ad Reverendissimum ac Amplissimum Patrem D. Garsìa de Loayasa Sacrae Romanae Ecclesiae Cardinalem Ludovicus Comesius Hispanus Sacrii Palatii Apostolici causarum Auditor salutem plurimam dicit.

Cum a diluvio illo Tyberis ad domum tuam Pater amplissime veluti ad Deucalionis navim confugissem, hic a tuis quamvis luculento ac liberali plane et regio apparatu (quo saepe soles studiosos excipere) acceptus essem, animo tamen dolebam miseram Urbis conditionem. Privatus enim eram gravissimo conspectu Patrum, quorum cottidiano colloquio ac communium studiorum commertio in curia et foro saepe fruebar. Carebam pulcherrimis illis Reipublicae muneribus, quae summis meis laboribus laudem mihi et gloriam afferre poterant. Carebam privatis studiis ac librorum meorum supellectile, quorum usu gravissimas curas levare consueveram. Videbam insuper furore Tyberis omnia in praeceps agi atque undis suffundi. Nec poteram   18 in tantis Reipublicae malis non vehementer dolere ac moestus esse, donec tu, Pater Optime, litteratorum columen, ab Exquiliis rediens sapientissimis tuis sermonibus ac dulcissima consuetudine moerorem animi sustulisti. Sic itaque post verba multa (ut fit) ultro citroque habita forte in sermonem alluvionum incidimus. Aderant ibi ex tuis periti multi qui contentiose quaedam Tyberis prodigia referebant. Tunc mihi, cui nihil erat hoc tempore in quo animum sublevarem, maior cupido incessit vetera revocare studia a quibus [A2v] me paululum forenses causae diverterant, et ludicra quaedam ad rem pertinentia forte gerris Syracusanis vaniora in ordinem redigere, ac tibi alioqui ingentibus curis obruto, levandi animi causa privatim dicare, non ea lege tamen, ut in publicum exeant. Nam neque talia sunt quae lucem habere mereantur. Neque rursus tanto candore polita ut peritorum lectione sint digna. Et si videri possent digna, tanta sunt celeritate congesta et tam modico temporis spatio, et illo quidem calamitoso confecta, quod cum ad emendationem ocium defuerit, reprehensione carere non poterunt. Utcunque sit, dabis veniam facilitati meae, nam cum tute mihi auctor audendi fueris, agnoscere foetum debes intempestivo partu obortum. Vale studiosorum decus et me, ut facis, ama.

[A3r] Romae pro foribus templi Sancti Ioannis Evangelistae e regione domus Reverendi Domini Thomae de Prato Datarii integerrimi.

19

C[AIUS] VIBIUS C[AII] F[ILIUS] RUFUS
SEX[TUS] SOTIDIUS SEX[TII] F[ILIUS] STRABO
LIBUSCID[IUS]
C[AIUS] CALPETANUS C[AII] F[ILIUS] STATIUS RUFUS
M[ARCUS] CLAUDIUS M[ARCI] F[ILIUS] MARCELLUS
L[UCIUS] VISELLIUS C[AII] F[ILIUS] VARRO
CURATOR[ES] RIPARUM ET ALVEI TYBERIS
EX S[ENATUS] C[ONSULTO] TERMIN[AVERUNT]

⚜

20

[A3v] Reverendissimo ac illustrissimo Domino Dom. Garciae de Loaysa Cardinali Oxomensi Franciscus Minitius Calvus salutat.

Facere non possum, Ampliss. Domine, quin tibi cum meo, tum vero eruditorum omnium nomine singulares gratias agam, qui libellum hunc de inundationibus Tyberis ab eximio et summae eruditionis viro Ludovico Comesio doctissime prudenterque conscriptum, per me typis excudi ac in lucem dari voluisti. Eoque me hercule magis studiosi omnes tibi debere fatebuntur, quo id invito auctore, qui commentarios ipsos tibi uni dedicaverat, tua de causa sunt adepti. Te enim, qui praeterquam quod inter coeteros Christianae Reipublicae cardinales maxime splendes et ab omnibus ob tuas praecellentes virtutes et praeclaras animi dotes vehementer commendaris, tanta praeterea apud Clementem VII Pontificem Maximum Caesaremque auctoritate polles, quanta hisce temporibus nemo, hac in re non modo perbenignum, verum etiam cunctis studiosis, quantum in te est, commodare illosque non mediocriter fovere ostendisti. Qui quidem, quod tibi duntaxat et eruditioni et non parvae oblectationi esse poterat, ad communem litteratorum omnium usum et commoditatem edendos ultro mihi libentissime dedisti. Atqui praeterea libellum hunc a plerisque legendum esse censeo. Nanque ad eximiam doctrinam atque scientiam, quam exinde lectores colligent, illud quoque accedet, quod adeo clare dilucideque maximae Tyberis alluviones, quantumque mali portendere consueverint, in eo describuntur, ut quisque diligenti horum commentariorum lectione facile intelligens, innumeras et gravissimas calamitates christianis omnibus ob corruptissimos vitae mores imminere, curet pro salute vitam vere Christianam induere. Ago igitur denuo gratias immortales, ornatissime domine, et quoniam huiusmodi salturari beneficio a te potissimum sumus affecti, et quod immortalitati florentis gloriae ipsius auctoris hoc pacto feliciter consuluisti. Vale et me inter tuos clientes adnumerare velis te etiam atque etiam rogo.

21

[A4r] Cautum est severissimo edicto Clementis VII Pontificis Maximi nequis praeter Franciscum Minitium Calvum intra proximum quinquennium commentarios hosce imprimat vel ab aliis temere forsan impressos vendat.

[A4v] *Ad Sanctissimum Clementem Septimum Pontificem Maximum Francisci Marii Molsae Epigramma*

Quod pelago aequarit tumidarum flumina aquarum
Tybris, et obsessa fluxerit Urbe minax,
Ne desponde animum, Clemens, dant omnia laeta
Haec tibi coeruleis stagna refusa vadis.
Sic tua non capient olim te regna, sed ingens,
Oceani aequabis finibus Imperium.

22

[Br] De Tyberis ortu, nomine et numine deque eius inundationibus et earum eventu per Ludovicum Comesium Sacri Palatii Apostolici causarum Auditorem et Sacrae Poenitentiariae Regentem

PARTICULA PRIMA:
DE ORTU, NOMINE ET NUMINE TYBERIS

Satis constat Tyberis flumen ex Apennino fonte defluens, apud antiquos multiplicis fuisse nominis. Erat tamen non modica contentio cuius potissimum ditionis esset, quo etiam nomine revenuncuparetur. Nam Ethruria Tyberim dicebat suum, quia oriebatur in Samnio, et negabat esse originis Latinae. Et quia Volturreni Imperii limes erat, ut inquit Fabius Pictor, Volturnum appellabat. Verum, quia Samnium oppidum iuxta mare et Tyberim colonia romana fuit, Roma ut suum vendicans Volturnum etiam appellabat. Error enim inde provenerat quia Volturni nomen variis de causis utrique genti pertinebat. Volturnus enim deus Tyberis erat, ut testis est Varro libro primo *De Lingua Latina*, quem Ethrusci ab eis habuisse nomen et originem contendebant. Vel ex Volturna regia Ethruscorum urbe, de qua Plinius libro tertio meminit; sive a Volturno, quod dicebatur Capua, quae sub ditione fuerat Ethruscorum, ut videre est apud Livium libro quarto *Ab Urbe condita* et Fabium Pictorem *De origine Urbis*; aut a Volturno fluvio, qui Ptolemaeo et Plinio testibus, oriens in Samnio et iuxta Capuam praeterfluens, mari mergitur; vel a Vertumno, qui erat princeps et municipalis deus Ethruriae, qui sicut Ianus in urbe pariter colebatur, ut Propertius auctor est quarto *Elegiarum* et Donatus explicat ex verbis Horatii *Epistolarum* libro primo.

Nam Vertumni numine factum est ut Roma, quae propter inundationes Tyberis palustris erat et ad habitandum incommoda, apta et idonea fieret. Nam factis Vertumno sacrificiis, Tyberis in alveum suum rediit, ut refert Fabius Pictor libro I *De aureo saeculo*. In tanta igitur vetustarum rerum contentione, Ethrusci nominis ambiguitatem tollere cupientes, Tyberim appellarunt Tuscum, qui etiam Tuscorum deus erat, ut Propertius elegia ad Vertumnum meminit. Sed labentibus deinde annis illa veterum Volturni denominatio in desuetudinem abiit et plu-[Bv]ra alia nomina sortitum est flumen, quorum seriem et proprietatem diffusius explicat Annius libro VII *Commentariorum* et Bocatius in libro *De fluminibus*, quorum praecipue tria ista fuerunt: Tybris, Albula et

23

24

Tyberis, ut ex Plinio et Marone Tortellius colligit. Illud tamen inter tot veterum altercationes, adeptus est laudis ac tantum gloriae ut inter mundi flumina carminibus vatum toto sit orbe celeberrimus. Nam et Xanthum atque Symoentem Graecorum memoria illustres superat teste Bocatio libro VII *Genealogiae* non solum prodigiorum eventu, quam vi quadam et potentia aquarum iuxta illud Ovidii II *Methamorphoseos:*

> *Cui fuit rerum promissa potentia Tybri;*   25

et libro IIII *Fastorum:*

> *Tuque futurae parens Tybri potentis aquae.*

Tenuis primo ortu, fluvius deinde quinquaginta fere auctus, in immensum evadit, ideo teste Plinio quarumlibet magnarum navium capax est, et rerum toto orbe nascentium mercator placidissimus, cuius alveus tantae profunditatis invenitur, ut dum obeliscus ille insignis C. Caesaris, qui hodie in Vaticano conspicitur, in urbem per ostia Tyberina traducendus esset, facta tunc aquarum dimensione, compertum fuit tantum aquae inesse Tyberi quantum Nilo, ve idem Plinius auctor est libro XXXVI. Hic aquarum incorrupto liquore dictus Sacer, adeo quod numen habere creditur. Et quamvis eius Numinis aestimationem Aeneas Silvius *Epistola* CIII variis deludat originibus, illud tamen certum   26 est veteres ob eius numinis reverentiam ad ripam eius aedificia ponere noluisse. Nam ad numen Tyberis etiam referunt quod virgo illa vestalis aquam ex Tyberi hauserit perforato vase, nec diffluerit. Simul etiam quod Chloelia virgo una ex obsidibus Porsene datis, frustrata custodes dux agminis virginum, inter tela hostium Tyberim tranavit incolumis, auctore Livio libro secundo. Inde Iuvenalis *Satyra* Sexta:

> *Imperii finem Tyberinum Virgo natavit.*

Et quod de Horatio Coclite iidem auctores testantur, ad numen etiam ascribunt quando praeciso ponte Sublicio dixit:

> Tyberine pater, te sancte precor haec arma et hunc militem propitio flumine accipias.

Neque hoc aliquis facile cavilletur, si dixerit Horatium Coclitem nandi peritum fuisse, cum potius Tyberis occulto numini, quod et Chloeliae virgini alioquin nandi imperitissimae adfuit,   27 ascribendum videatur. Nam si Pamphilicum mare in se divisum, iter terrestre praebuit Alexandro Magno et militibus suis in Persarum imperium irruentibus, [B2r] quod olim mare rubrum praestiterat Moysi, ut de utroque auctor est Iosephus libro II *De antiquitatibus Iudaeorum* capitulo ultimo, cur putandum non est hoc idem fieri in Tyberi posse? Et quod Alexandro contigit alioqui tyranno, quis Horatio Cocliti patriae propugnatori non evenisse putet? Quis enim numini cuidam occulto Tyberis non ascribat, quod tenui fluens alveo Romulum et Remum ad ripam servarit incolumes? Quod etiam ex restagnantibus aquis Tyberis insula sit effecta? Sed nusquam magis mortalium natura contumacior fuit quam in miraculis credendis. Utcunque se res habeat, nos ex alio aliam numinis significationem colligimus, videlicet quod Tyberis aquae, praesertim quae intra urbis moenia continentur, incorruptae ubique serventur, ut eundem aquae gustum in ultimas terras profectis retineant, quem Romae habere soleant; sive religione quadam urbis tot martyrum sanguine consecratae, aut occulta naturae vi, seu quod Tyberis paludibus et stagnis minime involvatur illud accidat, haud satis compertum est, nisi velimus ad aliam rationem referre, quod aqua Tyberis etiam purgatissima continuo arenam vel limum pro matrice retineat occulta et subtili naturae commixtione, quo fit ut diutius et ubique incorrupta servetur. Nam probabili experimento compertum est aquas, quae arenis non commiscentur, facile putrescere. Quinimmo quae sui natura ob arenarum defectum corrumpuntur. Si arenis miscenatur, facile conservari. Refert enim Procopius libro III *De bello Persico,* quod cum Antonia Bellisarii uxor cognosceret aquas omnes, quae iuxta Aetnam decurrunt facile corrumpi, iussit vasa vitrea impleri eaque in imo navis ubi sol minime penetrabat poni et arenis involvi, asseribus hinc inde locum muniens. Quo quidem experimento factum est ut aqua incorrupta conservaretur, et suave poculum navigantibus praeberet; nam et vinum et oleum fecibus vel amurca diutius conservari, eisdem etiam deficientibus extemplo corrumpi, periculo iam compertum est.

Quamobrem putandum est veteres aquis Tyberis sacrum tribuisse honorem. Nam ad religionem et numen pertinere arbitrabantur, si prius quam sacra inirent, matutinis temporibus ter aqua Tyberis immergerentur et expiarentur, ut refert Iuvenalis *Satyra* VI, dum inquit:

Ter matutino Tyberi mergetur, et ipsis
Vorticibus timidum caput abluet.

Et Persius *Satyra* Secunda:

Haec sancte ut poscas, Tyberino in flumine mergis
Mane caput bis terque, et noctem flumine purgas.

[B2v] Ut etiam Apuleius meminit. Huc pertinet illud Horatii libro   29
secundo *Sermonum*:

Frigida si puerum quartana reliquerit, illo
Mane die, quo tu indicis ieiunia, nudus
In Tyberi stabit. Casus medicusve levarit
Aegrum, ex praecipiti mater delira necabit
In gelida fixum ripa, febrimque reducet.

Inter has tamen naturae dotes saevus alioquin et tyranno similis
fluvius, qui nantes interdum rapit et diris vorticibus absorbeat
peritissimos, cuius inundationes, cum semper fuerint noxiae,
a veteribus etiam prodigii loco sunt habitae; quamvis Plinius
diversa sententia *Naturalis Historiae* libro III dixerit Tyberis subitis
incrementis, religiosum verius quam saevum, qui parum eius
saevitiam expertus fuerit. Nam inter vigintitria Tyberis epitheta,
quae ex varia lectione Ioannes Ravisius Textoris congessit, Rapidum
veteres Tyberim appellabant sive Rumon, quasi inundationibus ripas
ruminans et exedens, ut Servius in VIII *Aeneidos* auctor est, ubi
etiam subdit quod in sacris Serra dicebatur. Unde Virgilius ibidem   30
de Tyberi loquens:

Et pinguia culta secantem.

Et Ovidius libro primo *Fastorum*:

Radit arenosi Tybridis unda latos.

Quod cum veterum exemplis, tum maxime miserabili nostrorum
temporum inundatione, acerbissime experti sumus, ut suo loco
dicetur. Sed quando huc deventum est, ut inundationum Tyberis
mentio fieret, operaeprecium perscrutandum erit, num veteres illae
inundationes, quae a Livio et antiquis auctoribus memorantur,
praestiterint recentioribus, quae ab ortu Christi contigisse dicuntur.
Res certe ambigua, obscura et parte ab utraque varia ac coniecturis
plena, quae cum plures sint et inter se pugnantes, ille clariorem nobis

huius negotii lucem dabunt, quae vehementiores ac magis probabiles iudicatae fuerint.

Coniecturae igitur, ex quibus persuaderi possunt inundationes veterum fuisse maiores, hae offeruntur. Prima quia constat olim campum illum, qui inter Palatium et Capitolium est, non satis fuisse idoneum ad habitandum propter inundationes Tyberis. Nam ob eam causam locus ille palustris erat et insalubrem emittebat aerem, 31   ut Fabius Pictor libro I *De aureo saeculo* auctor est. Ex quo igitur ad illum locum aquae Tyberis attingebant, facile deprehendi potest maiores fuisse inundationes illas veteres quam recentiores, quod etiam manifesto argumento probatur. Nam aquae Tyberis tunc etiam uberiores [B3r] et copiosiores fuisse constat et ita copiosiores, ut mirandum sit cur accedentibus imbribus etiam montes ipsos non attingerent. Nam legimus Claudium Caesarem magna impensa, plura flumina, fontes et lacus ad Tyberim derivasse, ad quem etiam praeter aquas ad ministeria sordida deputatas, decem et novem aquaeductus defluebant, ut Sextus Ruffus auctor est, quos deinde 32   collabentes[1] Theodoricus Ostrogottorum rex, ab iniuria vetustatis vindicavit.

33   Ex quibus quatuordecim adhuc tempore Sylverii papae fluebant, donec eos barbarorum manus Vitige duce interciderunt. Quorum aliquos Adrianus Papa Primus magna impensa restituit, ut Damasus et Platina testantur. Quarum quidem aquarum congeries, quae magna fuerat, ad Tyberim decurrebat, ad quem etiam septem illi rapidissimi amnes, quos torrentium modo ut cuncta raperent in subterraneas cloacas Marcus Agrippa demitti iusserat, derivabantur, ut Strabo et Cassiodorus libro IIII *Epistolarum* meminerunt, adeo ut dicat Plinius libro XXXVI Urbem totam fuisse pensilem et subtus navigabilem, ut si quis diligenter aestimaverit aquarum abundantiam 34   in publico, balneis, piscinis, domibus, euripis, hortis, suburbanis villis, spacioque advenientium, structosque arcus, montes perfossos, convalles aequatas, fatebitur nihil magis fuisse mirandum in toto orbe terrarum.

In tanta igitur aquarum ubertate putandum est Tyberim magis olim fuisse tumidum, plenum, et aquarum multitudine profundum, quam modo sit, ut facilius ac copiosius inundaret. Accedit riparum

---

1.   Corrected from "collabentess."

eius coangustatio, nam in tam plena et populosa urbe, non putabant expedire, ut tanta aquarum congeries pro libito divagaretur, unde Marcus Agrippa eius alveum compressit. Et Aurelianus Imperator, validissimo muro lateritio utrinque usque ad mare structo, Tyberim intra ripas coercuit, cuius operis adhuc extant vestigia.

Quis igitur inficiabitur, si tam pleno et tumenti fluvio intra riparum fines coarctato, imbrium aquae accederent, non in maximas et mirabiles prorumpere inundationes? Hinc merito iam verum fuisse credimus quod dixit Plinius tantum tunc aquae continuisse Tyberim quantum Nilum. Quamobrem, ut moderarentur eius inundationes et vis illa ingens aquarum comprimeretur, saepe actum in Senatu legimus. Super qua re ut creditur causam Cicero dixit apud consules et decem legatos. Itaque vetus fuit querela, quae nunquam maior suborta fuit quam Tyberii Imperatoris tempore. Nam ut primo libro refert Cornelius Tacitus:

> Eo anno continuis imbribus auctus Tyberis magnam hominum et aedificiorum stragem edidit, et ita prorupit quod Romanorum [B3v] omnium mentes turbaverat, adeo quod Asinius Gallo ob eam causam censuerat Libros Sybillinos adeundos, ni Tyberius vetuisset; constitutis ad hoc negocium duobus viris Atteio Capitone et Q. Aruntio, qui fluminis impetus cohercerent curarentque ut flumina verterentur et lacus per quos augescit; auditaeque tunc in Senatu fuerunt municipiorum et coloniarum legationes orantibus Florentinis, ne Clanis solito alveo dimotus in amnem Arnum transferretur idque ipsis perniciem afferret. Congruentia his Interamnates disseruere pessum ituros foecundissimos Italiae campos, si amnis Nar (id enim parabatur) in rivos diductus, superstagnavisset. Nec Reatini silebant, Velinum lacum, qui in Narem effunditur, obstrui recusantes, quippe in adiacentia erupturum: optime rebus mortalium consuluisse naturam, quae sua ora fluminibus, suos cursus, utque originem ita fines dederit. Spectandas etiam religiones sociorum qui sacra, et lucos, et aras patriis amnibus dicaverunt, quin ipsum Tyberim nolle prorsus accolis fluviis orbatum minore gloria fluere. Seu preces coloniarum, seu difficultas operum, sive superstitio valuit, Senatus in sententiam Pisonis concessit, qui nihil mutandum censuerat.

35

Haec Tacitus. Ex cuius verbis apparet satis quantum negocii dederint Populo Romano inundationes Tyberis, quamvis in montibus maiori ex parte habitarent. Ut hinc facile coniectari liceat illorum temporum inundationes maiores et altiores fuisse his, quae nostra aetate contigerunt. Nam credendum est Traianum eam ob causam magnam illam fossam iam prius ab alio ceptam ad mare producere voluisse, ut tumentes aquae Tyberis exitum haberent, ut de Nilo fecisse Darium et Ptholemaeum reges auctor est Diodorus. Et non alio studio Iulium Caesarem motum credimus, ad emittendum

36 Fucinum lacum, viam muniendam a mari supero per Apennini dorsum usque ad Tyberim, nisi ut inundationes essent leviores et facile perferrentur. Haec sunt argumenta quae partem istam tueri videntur.

Sed ex diverso quod inundationes nostrorum temporum antiquioribus praestent, illud argumentum facit quod exacta illa Tyberis expurgandi cura cum imperio abiit. Neglectis enim miris illis operum substructionibus, alveus etiam Tyberis cepit negligi, adeo ut, si verum fateri volumus, nostra aetate bonam eius alvei partem, via quae dicitur Iulia, et aedificia novissime in utraque ripa, fabricata occupent. Et quod reliquum est coangustari alvei ita ruinis pontium et aedificiorum ac totius urbis excrementis oppletum est, ita lapidum fragmentis et arenis refertum, ut remorato aquarum cursu mirandum sit cur saepius non inun- [B4r]det, cum saepissime olim laxiori alveo ac optime purgato inundaret. Conlachrymabis si nunc Tyberim inspicias, quae propter alvei purgati latitudinem ac facilem et expeditum cursum veteres lubricum appellabant. Positi enim fuerant in hanc rem a senatu et Augusto curatores, ut nuper effossi lapides iuxta pontem Vaticanum ostendunt. Nam, ut refert Suetonius Tranquillus,

> Roma prius fuerat inundationibus obnoxia, ad quas cohercendas Augustus Tyberis alveum laxavit et repurgavit completum olim ruderibus et aedificiorum prolapsionibus.

Sed hodie quando periit illa cura, contrario nomine lentum Tyberim seu tardum vel morosum appellabimus, adeo quod facile intumescat, ut Aureliani tempore contigit, ubi propter rudera et ruinas urbis tumens et tardus erat, quam quidem alvei tumentis

37 tarditatem magnanimus princeps effosso vado Tyberis sustulit,

ut auctor est Flavius Vopiscus. Quod et Cyrus Persarum rex de Sinde fecit. Nam cum aquarum copia esset tardus et ea de causa inundationibus noxius, plurimis factis ductibus abscidit. Numero eos fuisse dicit Herodotus centies quater et decies sex ad eamque demum exiguitatem redactum, ut sicco pervaderetur pede; et idem de Nilo, qui saepe prius inundabat, Osirim fecisse legimus, ut refert Diodorus. Lacum etiam effodit Myris rex apud Memphim supra urbem ambitu stadia trecenta et sexaginta profundum cubitos L, quo Nilum quando acrius insurgeret, exciperet et eius incrementa confunderet. Sic Claudius apud Fucinum lacum montem perfodit et aquae nimietatem obduxit in fluvium et eodem respectu de lacu Velino factum fuisse per Marcum Curiorem putandum est. Sicut etiam Caesar fossas quam plures facere apud Hylerdam instituerat, quibus partem aliquam Sicoris fluvii averteret; ad Euphratem etiam ne tecta urbis diriperet, praeter moles, quibus cohercerentur, nonnullos etiam lacus, qui excipiant vim fluminis, addidere. Et ob eam causam Tarquinius Priscus Tyberis alveum direxit. Et deinde Marcus Agrippa aedilis, quia alveus Tyberis adhuc obliquus erat, magis rectum fecit et alveum mutavit, magnisque molibus saxorum in utraque ripa locatis solidavit. Nam, ut scribunt Servius in VIII *Aeneidos* et Pomponius, Tyberis sub Capitolio inferebat sinum qui pertingebat radices Palatii ubi erat ficus Ruminalis, ad quam eiecti sunt Romulus et Remus. Ibi postea fuit Circus inter Palatium et Capitolium ubi etiam Lupercal, ut tradit Fabius Pictor libro II. Nimirum igitur si eius inundationes tunc viderentur ea de causa pernitiosae, quas Vertumnus factis sacrificiis avertit secundum Servium, mutato deinde alveo, non ita urbi incommodus [B4v] fuerat, licet aliquando inundaret. Nostra vero aetate, cum in plano et iuxta Tyberim nova Roma aedificata sit, cura etiam fluminis penitus neglecta sit, ut coangustato eius alveo et ad strictas et angustissimas fauces redacto, ruderibus etiam et ruinis pleno, faciles et magis damnosas emittat inundationes, ut merito credendum sit veteribus longe fuisse maiores. Constat enim ex lapide effosso apud domum Reverendissimi Patris Domini Thomae de Prato, qui nunc merito datarium agit, alveum antiquum Tyberis se ad illum protendisse locum.

38

39

Expendet igitur amicus lector ex istis coniecturis sibi invicem adversantibus, quae nam probabiliores sint ad suadendam alteram partem; quarum iudicium non temere proferam, cum satis fuerit coniecturas ostendisse, quibus rem dubiam reddiderimus. Nam dubitarem suspectus haberi iudex si stante recentiori ac acerbissima inundatione Tyberis, qua gravissima damna sum passus, iudicarem antiquas inundationes fuisse maiores quas nunquam viderim. Nec percipere nisi coniecturis possum, maxime cum ante oculos obversentur praesentia damna mortalium nunc primum postrema ista inundatione illata. Operae precium igitur erit secundo loco eas omnes aquarum alluviones, quae per omnes aetates Romae contigerunt, adnumerare, ut ex casibus adversis praeteritorum temporum praesentia incommoda consolemur et quasi socia fortunae vice leviter feramus.

SECUNDA PARTICULA TRACTATUS: DE INUNDATIONIBUS TYBERIS

Restat nobis in tanta rerum serie eas omnes inundationes quae a veteribus et recentioribus memorantur ordine suo digerere. Res profecto acerbitatis et laboris plena, sed quae plurimum habeat iucunditatis. Nam ita natura comparatum est, ut plus in adversis hominum casibus et aerumnis, quam in prosperis eorum successibus perlegendis homines oblectentur, cui quidem oblectationi consulemus facile, si rem ipsam quae longiore apparatu indigere videbatur, perstringamus breviter. Sic itaque fiet ut cum insignes duntaxat et notabiles Tyberis alluviones describemus, exiguas et minus notabiles omittamus, quae nullum negocium dederunt aut admirationem Populi Romani et eas tantum describemus quas Tyberis intulit. [Cr] Nam neque maris incrementa plurima vel inundationes omnium fluminum a quibus quaedam provinciae nomen acceperunt, ut Acaiae, persequimur, quamvis plurimae sint, quae a prodigioso Nilo et Pado et Danubio toto orbe terrarum clarissimis fluminibus illatae memorantur. Sufficiet autem nobis in tanta operum congerie eas tantum alluviones deligere, quae ad institutum nostrum pertinere arbitramur.

INUNDATIONES TYBERIS ANTE CHRISTI ADVENTUM

Prima Inundatio
Prima omnium inundatio quam Tyberis protulit, veterum memoria illa fuit quae bellum inter Veientinos et Populum Romanum pene

40

diremit aut saltem magnitudine sua distulit. Nam, ut refert Livius libro IIII *Ab Urbe condita*, Tyberis super ripas effusus, agros maxime ruinis villarum vastavit, simul Equos triennio ante accepta clades prohibuit Volanis suae gentis populo praesidium ferre etc. Ex cuius verbis facile coniectari potest non adeo parvi momenti alluvionem illam fuisse quae potuerit maiestatem illam principum Populi Romani a negociis publicis avocare.

Secunda Inundatio

Sed neque minoris momenti fuit illa Tyberis inundatio quae ab eodem Livio *Secundi Belli Punici* libro III refert. Nam eo anno inquit quo Q. Fabius Maximus et Marcus Marcellus consulatum inibant, aquae magnae et nives fuerunt, quibus factum est ut Tyberis agros inundaret cum magna strage tectorum, pecorumque et hominum pernicie. Contemplari licet ex verbis Livii miseram illorum temporum conditionem quando ardentissimis bellorum facibus tota fere Italia conflagrabat. Instabat enim tunc ad portas Annibal barbarus et gloriosus hostis nomen extinguere romanum. Et ne uno tanto malo civitas doleret, addidit se sociam Tyberis alluvio plena damnis et tristissimi eventus. Sed vicit tandem virtus et constantia populi romani posteros ad sufferenda fortiter pericula monens.

Tertia Inundatio

41

Inferrem hic libens aliam aquarum infusionem, de qua idem Livius meminit libro X *Belli Punici,* quae Circum Flamineum inundavit, nisi vidissem ex eo levem fuisse existimatam, quod populum romanum ad ludum invitavit. Nam extra Portam Collinam ad aedem Erycinae Veneris, tunc ludi Apollinares parati fuerant, et quod plerique moero- [Cv] rem et luctum adduxisset, illis plausum et laetitiam attulit. Sed tam secundae fuerant illis temporibus et prosperae Romanorum res quod tristia alioqui prodigia adiuvante fortuna, verterentur in bonum.

Quarta Inundatio

Nam quaedam alia fere similis alluvio aquarum temporibus Q. Metelli consulis occurrens prodigii loco habita fuit. Sic enim alternat fortuna vices ut eandem rem pro temporum conditione mutet. Nam si Livio credimus libro V *De bello macedonico,* aquae ingentes eo anno effecerunt ut Tyberis inundaret omnia plana urbis et plurima

42

aedificia circa Portam Flumentanam secum traheret; putandum est, si ex praesentibus futura coniicimus, maximum urbi detrimentum attulisse. Nunquam enim Tyberis effluxit, quod non portenderet aliquod malum memorabilem.

Quinta Inundatio

Sed inter coeteras aquarum colluviones illa nos magis in admirationem trahit, quae temporibus Cn. Domitii consulis adeo Tyberis alveum opplevit, ita tumentem reddidit ut infestiore quam priore impetu illatus urbi duos pontes et aedificia multa everterit ac in agris pecora abstulerit, villarum stragem ediderit. Et tanta fuit imbrium copia ut saxum ingens, sive imbribus seu motu terrae leniore quam ut alioquin sentiretur labefactatum, in vicum Iugarium ex Capitolio prociderit multos opprimens, quae inter magna prodigia refert Livius eodem libro.

Sexta Inundatio

Et quamvis illa Tyberis inundatio magis infesta videri posset, quae Cn. Manlio consule eo anno duodecies urbem inundavit auctore Livio libro VIII *Belli macedonici*, ista tamen de qua proxime diximus, coeteris omnibus fuit praestantior, quae tantam secum calamitatem tulerit, tantam hominum stragem et aedificiorum ruinam, ut, si verbis exprimenda foret, nulla sane maior confingi posset alluvio. Nam quae vis aquarum tanta esse potuit ut pontes duos, qui magnis structi molibus erant, everterent? Nisi dicamus Sublicium pontem, qui unus ex eversis fuit, ligneum fuisse, ut nullo negotio everti posset. Sed hoc falsum est, quoniam si recensemus tempora, Sublicius pons, quem primum omnium Ancus Martius ligneum fecit, ut referunt Livius et Plinius, eius constructionis rationem reddentes, tempore huius inundationis, iam lapideus erat. Illum enim lapideum fecerat Aemilius Laepidus, praetor a quo nomen postea sortitus fuit, ut Pomponius Laetus, Fabricius Varranus, Albertinus Volaterranus et recentiores in collectaneis urbis meminerunt, quamvis Domitius Calderinus, Mancinellus et quidam neoterici gramma-[C2r] tici in hoc hallucinati fuerint super illo versu Iuvenalis *Satyra* VI:

43

> *Cum tibi vicinum se praebeat Aemilius pons.*

Qui dictus ante fuerat Sublicius, postea Tyberis inundationibus laesus, a Tyberio Caesare restitutus fuit. Deinde Antoninus Pius

44

marmoreum fecit, unde pons marmoratus usque in hodiernum diem dictus est, quem iterum everterat inundatio Tyberis sub Adriano I, cuius ruina adhuc conspicitur eo riparum Tyberis loco ad quem naves undique venalia vina important. Apparet igitur non levem fuisse illam aquarum copiam, quae pontem illum firmissimis basibus et fornicibus structum evertere potuit.

Alter ex duobus collapsis pontibus creditur ille quem ad portam Triumphalem apud aedem S. Spiritus collapsum cernimus, qui Vaticani pons vel secundum Iosephum libro VII *De captivitate* 45 *iudaica* Triumphalis dicebatur, per quem soli nobiles transire solebant. Quantae firmitatis fuerit pons ille, fundamenta quae adhuc extant satis demonstrant, non tamen usque adeo firma ut vim tantae inundationis sustinere potuerint. Potuit tamen Adriani pons, qui hodie dicitur S. Angeli, impetus illos recipere, cum sit opus omnium operum, quae homines fecerunt, validissimum. Dubitavit tamen Albertus libro X *De re aedificatoria* capitulo VIII firmitatem 46 illam diutius posse inundationibus Tyberis resistere. Nam stipitibus et ramis quos ex agris alluviones arripiunt, pilas annuis molestiis onerant et fauces arcus multa ex parte obturatas reddunt, fit ea re, ut aquae intumescant atque inde ex alto praecipites et molesti vortices corruant et convergantur et sic pilarum puppim subruant, molemque operis perturbent. Hactenus Albertus. 47

Cuius quidem vaticinii eventum novissima inundatione Tyberis experti sumus, nam obturatis prius duobus arcubus sub aedificio arcis Sancti Angeli, ita in eum hac postrema inundatione aquae conglomeratae impetum fecerunt ita sub arcto transitum veluti facto agmine pugnarunt, ut convulsa operis parte cum adhaerentibus aedificiis privatorum totus fere pons concussus fuerit. Eundem pene impetum cum pari iactura sustinuit Ianiculensis sive Aurelius pons, qui nunc dicitur Sixti. Nam licet eius arcus coeteris sint protentiores et ampliores et ita aquarum multarum capaces, tanta tamen in hac postrema quam sub Clemente VII Pontifice Maximo. vidimus inundatione fuit aquarum copia ac 48 tanta vis, ut nisi prius evulsis pontis radicibus a latere sinistro aquae sibi aditum facerent, dubitandum erat ne pontem secum traherent, de qua quidem inundatione inferius suo loco dicemus. Nam satis fuit ab effectu ostendisse inundationem illam magnitudine et aquarum abundantia coeteris omnibus fuisse maiorem [C2v].

Septima Inundatio

Magna etiam et insolens fuit inundatio illa quae sub Augusto contigisse memoratur. Nam, ut refert Aeneas Silvius *Epistola* CIII ubi Danubii incrementum scribit, Tyberis eo tempore supra littus Ethruscum excrescens monumenta Numae Pompilii regis templaque Vestae contigit ut, si verbis Horatii *Ode Secunda* fides adhibenda est, nulla maior Tyberis inundatio fuerit, ac proinde opinandum est Augustum animum longe maioribus curis obrutum, ad hoc unum negotium direxisse. Nam, ut refert Tranquillus, Urbem inundationibus obnoxiam excoluit et ad cohercendas inundationes Tyberis alveum laxavit.

Octava Inundatio

Sed neque levior fuit inundatio quae Tyberii Imperatoris tempore contigit. Nam, ut refert Tacitus libro primo, eo anno continuis imbribus auctus Tyberis magnam hominum et aedificiorum intulit stragem, adeo ut toti fere Italiae negotium dederit, de quo superius libro primo mentionem fecimus.

INUNDATIONES POST CHRISTI ADVENTUM

Nona Inundatio

Inter maiores quoque Tyberis inundationes, referenda est illa de qua Tranquillus meminit in vita Ottonis, quae usque ad vigesimum ab urbe lapidem ruina aedificiorum viam praeclusit. Tunc enim papa Linus erat, a quo sub pontificum nomine quae sequentur inundationes persequemur. Ortus enim iam fuerat christianae religionis iubar Christus, a quo veluti a renovato mundo initium annorum capiemus, ut sic res ipsa dilucidius percipi ac intelligi possit.

Decima Inundatio

Anacleti romani pontificis temporibus, Tyberis etiam in immensum crevit et multas aedes demolitus est, quae quidem inundatio multorum malorum pronuncia fuit. Nam et terraemotus multis locis, fames et pestilentia subsecutae fuerunt, quibus malis Traianus tunc imperator exquisitis undique remediis pro viribus obviavit et subvenit. Statuitque deinde, teste Rivalio, ne domorum altitudo sexaginta pedes excederet ob ruinas faciles et sumptus, si quando talia evenirent, nimios.

Undecima Inundatio 50

Illa tamen quae temporibus Adriani Imperatoris tantis fuit comitata malis, non tam ex aquarum violentia, quam ex prodigiorum uno tempore [C3r] contingentium euentu, inter memorabiles inundationes referri potest. Nam, ut Aelius Spartianus meminit in eius vita, fuerunt illis temporibus cum inundatione Tyberis fames ac pestilentia, ex quibus plures civitates vastatae fuerunt. Inciderat enim ista inundatio intra CXIX et CXXIX annos ab ortu Christi, inter pontificatum Alexandri et Sixti primorum pontificum romanorum. Nam vivente adhuc Adriano Caesare duo isti pontifices suo quisque ordine electi obierunt.

Duodecima Inundatio.

Acerbior tamen in eodem genere videri potuit alia aquarum congeries quam refert Iulius Capitolinus in Antonio Pio, quae anterioribus denuntiata prodigiis initium maiorum portentorum fuit. Nam inundationem illam praecesserat fames, Circi ruina, terraemotus et incendium quo Romae trecentae quadraginta insulae vel domus absumptae sunt praeter Narbonensem civitatem et Anthiochensem oppidum cum carthaginensi foro, quae uno tempore conflagrarunt. Post vero inundationem Tyberis apparuit stella crinita et puer biceps atque mulier uno partu quinque pueros enixa. In Arabia vero visus serpens iubatus solito maior, qui se a cauda medium devoravit. Et ordeum illo tempore in culminibus arborum natum, terrorem incussit. Itaque his talibus tantisque prodigiis inundatio uno tempore comitata, locum memoriae fecit. Sederat illo tempore in sede Petri 51
Telesphorus pontifex sub anno Salutis Christianae CXXXIX quo tempore incidit, ut dicit Platina, ista Tyberis inundatio.

Decimatertia Inundatio

Nec etiam praetermittenda est illa Tyberis effusio, quae ab eodem Iulio Capitolino in M. Antonio refertur, quae felicitatem imperatoris et securitatem eius interpellavit. Nam post illam inundationem, quae gravissima fuit ac aedificiis urbis et animalibus multa damna intulit, fames, bella gravissima et pestilentia secutae fuerunt, adeo quod cadavera vehiculis sarracisque fuerint exportata, quibus malis nisi obviasset pius et magnanimus princeps actum esset de urbe, ut idem auctor non uno tantum loco latius prosequitur, mirandum est tamen quod tam varia et remissa fuerit illorum temporum historia. Nam neque Damasus neque Platina, qui diligentius historiam summorum pontificum contexuerunt, de hac ista inundatione nec prodigiorum uno tempore contingentium multitudine meminerunt. Utcumque sit, accidit ista alluvio intra annos CLX et CLXVIII Salutis Christianae.

Decimaquarta Inundatio

Sed quis cladem illam tam multis auctoribus celebratam, quam Ty-[C3v] beris inundatio intulit Pelagii tempore, siccis poterit oculis pertransire? Refert enim Paulus Diaconus libro XVIII per ea tempora multis locis graves inundationes fuisse adeo ut Noe diliuvium renovatum crederetur. Nam in finibus Venetiarum et Liguriae seu caeteris regionibus Italiae factae sunt lacunae possessiones cum magno interitu hominum et animantium, destructa itinera, dissipate viae, tantumque tunc Athesis fluvius excrevit ut circa Basilicam Sancti Zenonis Martyris, quae extra Veronensis urbis muros sita est usque ad superiores fenestras aquae pertingerent, licet sicut Beatus Gregorius postea papa libro III *Dialogorum* scripsit in eandem basilicam aqua minime introiverit. Urbis quoque eiusdem Veronensis muri magna ex parte eadem sunt inundatione subrupti. Portendisse ferunt innundationem illam urbis Veronensis lachrimabile incendium, quod postea subsecutum fuit.

Subdit idem auctor: In hac diluvii effusione in tantum apud urbem Romam fluvius Tyberis excrevit ut aquae eius super muros urbis influerent et maximas regiones occuparent. Tunc per alveum eiusdem fluminis cum multa serpentum multitudine draco etiam magnae miraeque magnitudinis per Urbem transiens usque ad mare discendit qui a fluctibus maris suffocati et ad littus repulsi foetore circumiacentes regiones infecerunt, ut etiam latius refert archiepiscopus florentinus in vita Gregorii. Ex qua quidem serpentum et draconis corruptione aquarum limique per concava urbis dimissi exhalatione gravissima pestilentia subsecuta est, adeo ut sternutatione homines interirent quae adeo populum afflixit, ut de tanta et tam inextimabili multitudine vix decimus quisque superfuerit. Primumque omnium Pelagium Pontificem Maximum et alioquin virum maxime venerabilem perculit et sine mora extinxit, adeo quod, nisi in tam acerba et tristi persecutione Gregorius tunc

Papa, omnium consensu electus, precibus et cilicio septiformique   53
letania occurrisset, vix unus vel alter superesset. Nam eo ipso die quo
supplicationes agerentur, unius horae spatio octingenti ex eis subito
vitam exhalarunt. Longum esset inaudita illorum temporum prodigia
recensere quae a praefatis auctoribus latius circa hoc negotium
divagantibus scribuntur. Incidit tamen inundatio ista, ut scribit
Palmerius in additamentis Eusebii in annum Salutis Christianae
DLXXXVI vel secundum alios CCCCCLXXVI, ut quidem
supputant in eo libro qui inscribitur *Fasciculus temporum* cui quidem
si ex integro danda sit fides vix tot horrenda et admiranda prodigia
ab initio mundi una aetate sicut hic uno tempore contigerunt.

Decimaquinta Inundatio   54
Sub Gregorio II Pontifice Maximo anno DCCXVII a partu [C4r]
Virginis, Theodosio adhuc imperante secundum computationem
Palmerii florentini, Tyberis insolenti auctu a Porta Flaminea in
urbem irruens, per septem dies auctore Platina maximum urbi
detrimentum et civibus damnum intulit. Nam eversis domibus ac
arboribus satisque erutis aquae per urbem denso agmine decurrentes
omnia concava urbis implevere et adeo incrementum fecerunt ut in
Lata via hominis magnitudinem excesserint, et ita excesserunt quod
a ponte Milvio usque ad gradus S. Petri lintribus sit navigatum. Res
dura et improvidis longe calamitosa quae ex eo acerbior iudicari
potest quia haec inundatio, a coelo veluti adiuta, manifesto prodigio
fuerat praenunciata. Visus enim ante fuerat in coelo cometes caudam
suam ad Septentrionem dirigens atque sub ipsa inundatione luna
ecclypsim passa usque ad mediam noctem, colorem sanguineum
prae se tulit, ut merito credendum sit, si Damasum sequimur,
inundationem istam muros urbis transcendisse. Quamobrem
Gregorius tam horrendas christianorum calamitates miseratus, ut
iram Dei mitigaret, supplicationes tota Urbe fecit.

Decimasexta Inundatio
Incidit in vigesimum Adriani Primi Pontificis Maximi annum
alia Tyberis inundatio insolens. Nam fluvialis aqua in torrentis
speciem per Flamineam Portam quae nunc dicitur Populi irruens,   55
portam ipsam a fundamentis evertit, ut auctor est Damasus et
Platina; deinde late longeque spaciata pontem Sublicium, quem alia

inundatione collapsum diximus et M. Antonius Pius marmoreum reddiderat, iterum evertit cum magna hominum et rerum strage. Multa praeterea aedificia urbis et armenta, arbores, et segetes in praeceps acta muros et turres urbis pro magna parte vastavit totaque fere urbs; quae cimbis fluvialibus adiuta fuit, egestatem contraxit, quibus pontificis iussu cibaria subministrata fuerunt pauperibus nequentibus in apertum exire omnique alioquin ministerio carentibus. Obfuit cataclysmus ille non tantum in praesens sed causa etiam fuit ut anno sequenti sit Romae frumenti inopia laboratum. Consolatus est civitatem eiusmodi clade affectam Adrianus pontifex multa multis donans ut calamitas illa minus sentiretur, moenia et turres urbis aquarum vi dirutas reficiens. Quid plura? Nihil in tanta rerum egestate Adrianus praetermisit, quod ad optimum principem pertineret.

Decimaseptima Inundatio

Tyberis quoque prodigiose totam Urbem inundasse fertur sub Nicolao Primo pontifice. Nam totam illam planiciem, quae a via Lata ad radices Tarpeiae Rupis, a via quoque Argentaria ad Aventinum ducit, ita occu-[C4v]paverat ut instare diluvium crederetur, qua inundatione aliqua loca illustria aquarum impetu disiecta fuere, ut quidam retulerunt. Multae etiam domus eversae, arbores et sata passim in praeceps acta, neque hoc semel, ut ait Platina, illo anno contigit, sed et Decembri mense iterum Roma est inundationem passa. Haec damna emendare vel delinire pontifex enixus nullum genus officii et pietatis omisit. Neque enim exhaustus pontifex maxima itineris impensa ac molestia et praecedentium prodigiorum terrore ac novitate quae destinaverat exequi poterat. Nam inundationem illam duo praecesserant secundum Palmerium horrenda prodigia. Triduo enim sanguine pluisse in Brixiensi fertur et in Gallia vis ingens locustarum orta senos pedes habentium foede omnia popularunt, donec ventorum impulsu in Britanicum mare propulsae fluctibus obrutae perierunt, quas deinde Oceani aestus ad littora pellens, foetorem aerem infecerunt corruptoque terrarum tractu pestilentia secuta est et fames ingens, adeo ut tertia fere hominum[2] pars consumpta fuerit. Inciderunt haec damna circa

56

---

2.   Corrected from "homnium."

annum Domini DCCCLXII, quamvis Matthaeus Palmerius ad
Eusebium ista in Adriani Secundi tempora conferat.

Decimaoctava Inundatio

Gravis etiam et satis acerba fuit vis illa aquarum quam Tyberis
in urbem intulit Gregorii Noni tempore, ut referunt Damasus,
Platina et Sabellicus. Qui supra modum excrescens, multa damna
mortalibus intulit et mox tam foeda ac dira pestilentia secuta fuit,
ut decimus quisque vix superfuerit. Linquebant enim dulces animas
spiritus vitales tabe sanieque confecti, quibus malis se comitem
addidit prodigium solis, cuius defectio tanta fuit quanta numquam
antea memoretur. Secutae deinde sunt inter pontificem et Romanos
difficiles ac hostiles contentiones quae saeculum illud triste et
acerbissima tempora reddiderunt, ut latius prosequuntur historici.

57

Decimanona Inundatio

Inter prodigiosas quoque Tyberis inundationes memoratur illa quae
notato secundum Platinam per excrescentiam Tyberis vaticinio,
mortem Nicolai Tertii Pontificis Maximi praedixisse fertur. Nam
adeo per id tempus Tyberis insolenter excrevit, ita tumens fuit, ut ad
Pantheon nunc Deiparae Virginis est id templum, aram maximam
quaternis et eo amplius supergressa pedibus sit fluminis alluvio,
fuitque hic annus Salutis duodecies centesimum atque octogesimum.
Secuta deinde Nicolai mors locum prodigio fecit. Nam cum is
alioquin cibi et potus continentissimus et voluptatis expers subita
morte periisset, cre-[Dr] ditum est vastam et exitialem illam Tyberis
aquarum proruptionem id portendisse.

Vigesima Inundatio

Annus agebatur Salutis Christianae MCCCCXXI, cum Martinus
V Pontifex Maximus oculos direxit ad aspectum miserabilis Urbis,
quae diuturnis schismatum seditionibus et tyrannorum furore,
fame, ferro, ac pestilentia fuerat devastata. Omnia enim squallebant
situ aedificia sacra foede disiecta, insignisque vastitas, coenosa
et squallida viarum facies, ac agrestis et barbara quaedam feritas
civitatem invaserat. Receptus itaque cum ingenti omnium plausu
sedulo dedit operam, ut brevi omnia in melius mutarentur. Iam laeta
erant omnia et ad pristinum candorem redacta, cum Tyberis circa
festum Sancti Andreae a Porta Flaminia in urbem irruens totam

58

urbis faciem inundavit et gravissima damna civibus intulit veteresque plagas renovavit. Remisit tamen vis illa aquarum biduum postquam fuerat invecta multaque sunt animalia illa alluvione in praeceps acta, cuius quidem inundationis altitudo conspicitur hodie apud templum Minervae lapide in hanc memoriam signato.

Vigesimaprima Inundatio

Sederat iam per plures annos in pontificatu discordiis civilibus actus Sixtus Quartus Pontifex Maximus, cum Tyberis mense Novembri supra ripas effusus multa accolis damna intulit. Plura sunt etiam animalia inundatione ista aquis obruta, quorum putrefactione gravis pestilentia secuta fuit. Tot deinde horrenda et admiranda prodigia illis temporibus contigerunt, secundum Vincentium et recentiores auctores, ut vix credi possent. Venti etiam adeo ingentes ut multa aedificia subverterent, quae omnia mortem pontificis portenderunt.

Vigesimasecunda Inundatio

Fuit hic alter annus ab Alexandri Sexti creatione, quando alpina flumina, veluti facta coniuratione, prodigioso auctu omnem fere terram quae intra Padum iacet et Alpes per partes inundarunt, cum multa hominum strage et pecorum pernicie. Eruperat enim primo vis illa aquarum in Bergomati agro et, veluti signum dans, totam illam Veronensium circumiacentem regionem Athesi inundante pari clade affecit. Neque vero hic finis malorum fuit sed patavinum inde agrum et omnem Carnorum oram eadem cataclysmi vis invasit. Nec multo post, Tyberis supra modo auctus, omnia plana Urbis ad radices montium inundavit, adeo ut in ecclesia Sancti Iacobi Hispanorum aqua hominis magnitudinem excesserit, ut marmoreo lapide scriptum legimus. Ex qua inundatione Roma gravissima damna est [Dv] passa et plura etiam aedificia aquarum violentia corruerunt. Sed in plena et opulentissima urbe nequicquam talis alluvio quamvis maxima mentes civium turbaverat. Auro enim undique affluebat Roma neque iam poterat nunc magnitudinem suam sustinere. In tanto igitur divitiarum excessu, in tam ampla rerum omnium abundantia, conveniens alioqui et opportuna fuit alluvio, sicuti infirmo sanguine multo ac adipe repleto phlobotomia. Solent enim plerunque prosperae ac nimium secundae res longe hominem a se avocare et, cum seipsum non intelligat, rerum omnium

Servatorem negligat atque contemnat. Bona igitur fuit alluvio, quae ad se hominem redire coegit, ac veluti stimulo adversitatis tactum, quae vera et iusta sunt agnoscere. Habuerunt tamen inundationes istae hoc plus admirationis, quod parum evidenti causa subita illa inundatio contigerit, quum ne pluvio quidem coelo, ut quidam aiebant, flumina crevissent, et quod dierum intervallo non uno sit die ea clades evagata.

Scio enim non defuisse qui fingerent molem istam aquarum ex imbribus Alpium provenisse decussaque vi ventorum arborum folia causam praestitisse, ut torrentes multi uno impetu in subiecta flumina praecipitati, insuetum fecerint incrementum. Sed sive haec fuit causa, sive alia magis occulta, insueta rei facies in prodigium versa est. Multi ad tumultuosum in Italiam Gallorum descensum, prodigium illud aquarum retulerunt, quo tempore et Alphonsus Iunior neapolitano regno excidit et Ferdinandus pater medio belli apparatu fato obiit. Alii ad aliam causam referebant. Nec desunt qui inundationem istam Tyberis in ultimos Alexandri annos conferant. Verum hoc parum negotii dabit, si tempora numerentur, quae pluribus locis Romae descripta leguntur. Nam in lapide tyburtino ecclesiae Sancti Iacobi sub anno a partu Virginis MCCCCVC nonis Decembris scribitur inundatio, quae relata ad tempora Alexandri, incidit in secundum eius pontificatus annum plus minus.

61–62

Vigesimatertia inundatio

Eram ego maiori otio scripturus cladem istam miserabilem tam multis calamitibus sociatam, quam Tyberis inundatio intulit anno salutis MDXXX. Sed crescentibus in dies curis et inter officia publica quotidianis actionibus, quae me vinctum penitus et occupatum tenent, futurum erat ut si hoc negocium in aliud tempus reiicerem, minus fortassis haberem otii. Dum igitur recens tanti mali est memoria, dum [D2r] animus adhuc in luctu est praesentis calamitatis, operae precium duxi rem ipsam quam absolutissime perstringere.

Illuxerat nobis Saturni dies infanda, quae octava mensis numeratur Octobris, in qua Tyberis solito alveo dimotus, aquarum montes traduxit in Urbem cum ingenti omnium admiratione et damno. Videbantur enim uno illo die elementa omia coniurasse. Fatigabat dulces animas pavor ingens ex ruentium aedificiorum crepitu. Percutiebat insuper miserorum pectora praeteritorum malorum recordatio, quorum adhuc recentes fuerant cicatrices. Iam alii ad vindictam scelerum immisisse Deum inundationem istam asserebant, indiciis quibusdam assertiones suas comprobantes, quod videlicet sereno coelo nec praecedentibus magnis imbribus irruperit tam ingens vis aquarum, quasi quod fontes abyssi dissolvi viderentur. Addebant ecclypsin solis et lunae, quae eodem gradu eodem etiam inundationis die contigerat. Alii vero istam naturali rerum cursui tribuebant. Simul etiam memorabant inundationem illam quae Benedicti XII tempore toto orbe naturaliter contigit, ut novissimi quidam retulerunt, quando nullis praecedentibus imbribus, terra sponte sua ruptis interioribus venis ad modum diluvii scaturientium aquarum edidit torrentes, quibus prope infinita damna mortalibus illata leguntur. Et iam lunae ecclypsin in alios retorquentes, ad eundem naturae cursum referebant astronomorum testimonio innixi, qui vi quadam et potentia lunae omnium rerum humorem dicunt commoveri. Sic igitur in varias ire sententias cogebat pavor et quae non poterant damna providendo tollere, altercando solabantur.

Iam aquae in immensum creverant, nec altercationibus locus erat, cum ante oculos obversarentur ruinae vicinorum tectorum et, quod acerbius fuerat, timentibus et cernentibus illas omnes fugiendi aditus praeclusi erant. Sola inedia in consolationem vitae relicta. Usque adeo improvida et misera mortalium corda invaserat timor, ut homines amentes viderentur et elingues, et quo minus loquebantur, tanto magis suspectum et horribile videbatur silentium. Putabant enim non loquentes inedia aut aquis interemptos. Nec eorum qui loqui poterant audiebantur nisi gemitus et lamentationes. In summa, omnia erant plena luctus et tristissimi aspectus.

Inceperat inundationis huius dare signum Tyberis ante meridiem et crescentibus magis aquis carptim omnes urbis concavitates et subterranea loca implebant, nec prius super terram videbantur quam sibi prius aditum per subterraneos meatus facerent. Multorum etenim inferio- [D2v] res seu subterraneae cellae impletae aquis fuerant, ad quarum aedium superficiem aquae minime pervenerunt. Postquam vero omnia urbis concava quasi per insidias et clanculum repleta aquis fuerant, maiori impetu coepit Tyberis per vias et regiones urbis pro libito divagari et aquarum torrentes immittere, quasi quod urbem a sedibus imis aquis obruere destinasset. Et primum impetum fecerunt in pontem Adriani, qui nunc dicitur Sancti Angeli, ubi pater Tyberinus duos illos pontis arcus alvei antiqui, qui sibi sub aedificio arcis praeclusi fuerant, repetere volens collectis undique aquis arcem circundat et factis cuniculis evertere tentat. Sed cum nihil profecisset, magno veluti furore percitus, flumina omnia, fontes et amnes in auxilium vocat.

Iam nox erat quando ad obsidionem pontis et arcis quinquaginta fere flumina, quibus Tyberis pater praeerat se illi[3] addiderant, praeter torrentes plures et rapidissimos amnes, qui certatim socia aquarum agmina iungebant. Tunc Tyberinus instructis vorticibus et aquarum turbinibus, Adriani pontem iterum magno murmure adoritur, tanto aquarum cumulo, tanta vi, tanta denique turbinum congerie, ut Oceanum saevientem putares. Cingit itaque pontem ab omni latere atque aquis tegit ac subversis eius subgrundiis et parietibus totam illam aedificiorum partem, quae ad radices pontis Nummularios respicit, magnis et profundis voraginibus dissipavit. Ab alia vero parte Pontem Transtyberinum, qui ab arce Sancti Angeli ad Palatium viam praestat, a fundamentis sustulit, id futurum ratus ut pontem Adriani, praesidiis quibus hinc inde subnixus erat sublatis, parvo negotio everteret. Sed cum incassum diu aquae certarent neque machina illa altis fundata molibus ac firmissimis constructa basibus expugnari posset, Tyberis veluti rubore suffusus, collectis denique aquis, maiori impetu viam quam dicunt Iuliam aggreditur.

Hic locus olim alveus eius erat, cuius latitudo ad turrim quam hodie appellant Sabellicam protendebatur, ut nunc ibi inventi lapides monstrant, a quo fuerat vulgi seu plebeiorum manu paulatim eiectus et ad angustissimas riparum fauces redactus, quem quidem alvei amissi locum licet olim inundationibus pluribus recuperare tentaret, nusquam tamen compos fieri poterat, adeo difficile videbatur providos et munitos detentores propellere. Simulato igitur et dilato in plures annos negocio, cum iam omnia tuta et secura essent ac longa oblivione sopita, destinat occupati alvei iniuriam ulcisci, et praeter flumina et torrentes, quos prius in sui auxilium traxerat, solem etiam et lunam conscia numina Divum invocat, qui ecclypsi praesentes ma-[D3r] ximum aquarum incrementum intulerunt.

65

66

67

---

3.   Corrected from "ilii".

68–69

Sic itaque tot et tantis praesidiis adiutus, Tyberis viam Iuliam aggreditur furens modo hic, modo illic, a fundamentis aedificia omnia concutiens, spumosoque aquarum cumulo oppositas trahebat gurgite moles. Iam domus praealta et decora Iuliani Cecii magno fragore lapsa a sedibus imis ruinam dederat. Ab alio vero riparum latere ingentia illa regum coenacula Augustini Chisii praealtis et magnis instructa molibus ornata columnis auro picturatisque lapillis illustria cum bona viridarii parte vorticibus convulsa tegebantur undis.

70

Sed inter plures alias tectorum ruinas, quas ne sim prolixior omittam, non erit silentio involvenda clades studiosi et honesti viri Eusebii, quae veluti aliorum ruina denunciata ac vicinarum aedium prolapsionibus praemonita, non potuit evitari. Huius enim viri domum Tyberis furore accensus, tanto aquarum impetu concussit, ita suffodit ac vorticibus furentibus revulsam in abyssum traxit ac hominem cum supellectile et familia tota voraginibus absorbuit, ut vix operis vestigia appareant; mirum dictu quod tantus fuerit hic aquarum impetus, tantus furor, ut tot aedificia everteret, adeo quod via Iulia inter famosas et conspicuas urbis vias quondam habita, nunc concussione Tyberis dehiscens, ita sit effecta infamis, ita aedificiorum ruinis deformata, ut a propriis eius inquilinis destituta, sit iam deserta.

71

Sic enim variat fortuna vices. Nam quis merito non contremiscat, quis non horreat cum viderit illius viae tam magna aedificiorum ac firma fundamenta ab utraque parte locata occultis et subterraneis aquarum cuniculis perfossa, corrosa, atque convulsa, et adeo concussa ut nulla ibi sit domus quae non fuerit lapsa aut signum ruinae dederit? O misera mortalium conditio! O inanes cogitatus nostri, quam fluxa et varia est rerum humanarum spes, quam mutabilis et caduca illarum confidentia, quam varii et acerbi illarum casus!

Fuerat Roma matutino illo die satis secura et rebus paulatim prospere succedentibus hilaris et laeta. Cum ecce brevi temporis spatio versa sunt omnia in luctum et mutata in speciem pallidae mortis. Nam ut senes ipsos, pueros trepidasque puellas omittam, pallebant adeo ora robustiorum iuvenum ut propriam eorum faciem non prae se ferrent. Detinebantur enim improvidi, domibus carcerati, torquebantur timore et fame et, quod acerbius videbatur, omnes fugiendi aditus aquis praeclusi fuerant. Quae unquam Barbarorum hostium obsidio, quae captivitas, quae denique direptio huic poterit comparari? Huius enim comparatione illorum captivitas, summa erat libertas. Fruebantur enim captivi libero et sereno coelo, isti vero usu omnium elementorum privati, inter ipsa elementa clausi tectis, inglo- [D3v] rii morte Tantalea peribant.

Deerat enim vinum quod atrox Tyberis undis perfuderat neque aderant alimenta ignis ut saltem misera et afflicta corpora[4] ipso marmore frigidiora paululum reficerent. Sed quid de aquis dicam? Que tabe sanieque confectae poculum sine morte dare non poterant. Neque rursus illis copia farris erat, cum adhuc prioribus calamitatibus exhausti, in diem viverent. In summa nunquam magis carmina illa divini Maronis afflictae Troiae, quam tunc Urbi luctuosissimae convenerunt:

> *Quis cladem illius noctis. Quis funera fando*
> *Explicet? aut possit lachrymis aequare labores?*
> *Urbs antiqua ruit, etc.*

72

Sed magis hominum mentes turbabat dulcissimorum coniugum et natorum separatio, quae pluribus casu quodam evenit. Fuerant enim multi, ut fit, extra domum profecti, qui repentinis aquarum incrementis septi, eo unde digressi fuerant redire non poterant neque alter ab altero per internuntium intelligere an viverent, et quod in alio quis facile suspicabatur, in seipso timebat. Augebat etiam moerorem terrae motus a multis denunciatus, qui etiam parum ante inundationem a nonnullis praesensus fuerat. Simul etiam turbabat mentes quod nonnulli asserebant mare nolle illam aquarum colluvionem recipere sed arenarum aggeribus et ventis obstare.

Sicque inter inediam et metum vita transigebatur, donec biduo post Tyberis seipsum colligens, respirandi spem dederat. Nec minus negotii dedit urbi aquarum recessus seu decrementum quam laboris et damni earum augumentum. Reliquerat enim nobis habitationes urbis infirmas, ruinam fere minantes ac squallore multo horridas, coeno limoque refertas, ad quas repurgandas ac pessulis et contignationibus retinendas reliquum paupertatis impendebatur. Securae deinde sunt post inundationem Annonae caritas et quaedam pestilentiae signa ac ingens futuri mali timor ac suspicio.

---

4.   Corrected from "corporra".

Quidam ad regnorum vel provinciarum mutationes detorquentes dicebant influxum illum, quem Astronomi in annum MDXXIIII calculaverant, in istum derivatum fuisse cum sub ecclypsi lunae nec praecedentibus multis imbribus et sereno coelo contigerit inundatio, hac ratione probantes quod multis locis flumina et lacus auctum fecerint. Padus enim per idem tempus agros inundans plura damna intulit. Et Timavus etiam fines suos egressus signum dedit. Et Oceanus insolitas et horribiles elationes fecit, quae ad Holandiam sequenti mense contigerunt, quibus civitates plures cum incolis fluctibus actae et hominum boumque labores infelicissime deperditi memorantur. Quibus malis [D4r] pontifex vere maximus condolens exquisitis undique remediis obviare conatus est. Sed cum per iniquam praeteritorum temporum conditionem et acerbam Tyberis ruinam exhausta omnia atque dissipata fuissent. Non potuit pius et clementissimus princeps ea quae animo destinaverat ex integro adimplere constituitis in hoc negotium viris qui curarent ne quid detrimenti civitas pateretur multis, multa secreto donans.

PARTICULA TERTIA: DE INUNDATIONUM EVENTU

Ardua quippe res est et viribus meis impar inundationum successus et prodigiosos earum eventus brevibus quibusdam doctrinae indiciis praescribere. Nam, si effectus potius et non magis rerum causas attingimus, labor supervacuus erit plus oneris quam laudis habens. Sin vero initia rerum et quid illa necessario prae se ferant disseramus, erit cognitu digna lectio et intellectu iucunda paululum tamen magis periculosa, cum ea sit res, quae ultra immensam librorum seriem naturalium etiam rerum exigat peritiam, quae in me exigua est, et ad similitudinem ingenii mei pusilla. Iuvabit tamen utcumque sit meipsum consuluisse et posteris initia quaedam rudis vetustatis reliquisse. Sed ne in immensum crescat oratio, rem ipsam aggredior.

Magna sane et involuta fuit apud antiquos et recentiores dubitatio de eventu alluvionum ductibus faet quid eadem aquarum effusiones portenderent. Nam ex eo difficultas ingeritur quod nemo eorum quae viderim inundationum causas reddidit, licet plures earum effectus historici enarrarint. Operaeprecium igitur erit illud ex integro persc[r]utari, ut ea quae hactenus tractata non fuerunt, brevi compendio dignoscantur. Inter coetera igitur damna, quae nobis

inundationes pariunt, tria presertim mala portendunt, quorum duo
nobis ex accidenti eveniunt. Tertium necessario quodam influxu et
aquarum inundantium propria natura contingit.

DEFORMATIO STRAGESQUE RERUM EX INUNDATIONIBUS
Primum igitur damnum est tectorum ruina, hominum et
iumentorum interitus atque arborum disiectio. Hoc nobis aquae ex
accidenti et non ex propria earum natura afferunt, quoniam proprio
hominum consilio et providentia malum hoc evitari potest. Evitabitur
aut hoc modo, si an- [D4v] te omnia vim et naturam fluminum
exploraverimus, qua cognita iuvabit eorumdem fluminum impetus
fossis derivare, eversionibus minuere, aggeribus, stipitibus, molibus,
sive contignationibus cohercere. Nam Traianus plures in id negotium
fossas variis in locis fodi iussit, ut Plinius Iunior non uno tantum
loco *Epistolarum* libro X meminit. Sic etiam Caesar eodem studio
ductus fossas quamplures apud Hilerdam instituerat, quibus partem
aliquam Sicoris fluvii averteret, et Semiramis, ut elatis Euphratis   76
alluvionibus modum poneret, non contenta lateritio asphaltum etiam
superinduxit aggeri crassum cubitos quatuor. Cyrus etiam Persarum
rex Gyndem factis ductibus ita abscidit, ita ad exiguitatem redegit,
ut quasi sicco pervaderetur pede, teste Herodoto. Apud tumulum
Haliactis in Sardis lacus est factus manu ad excipiendas alluviones.
Lacum etiam effodit Myris apud Memphin, teste Herodoto, quo
Nilum exciperet acrius saevientem. Idem ad Euphratem factum fuisse
legimus. Nam Nitocris apud Mesopotamios Euphratem cursu nimio
concitatum retardavit curvis et tortuosis ductibus, ut idem auctor
scribit. Ex Nilo etiam Ptolemaeus cum navigaret, fossam aperiebat,   77
ut vis fluminis coherceretur, enavigata claudebat, teste Diodoro.
Accedent ad ista cura alvei et purgatio ruderum et prolapsionum, ut
exitum aquarum praebeat facilem. Nam, si ea negligantur, facile fit
ut sic cumulatis truncorum ramis et accrescentibus in dies arenis et
lapidibus, alveus sese attollat et petulantibus vorticibus ac ruentium
undarum vi aedificia evertat et convergatur et quandoque dimisso
priori et antiquiori alveo, ut Meander et Euphrates saepe fecerunt,
alio deflectat. Neque hic exigimus magnificam illam et sumptuosam
veterum Romanorum substructionem de qua quaedam de libro
I diximus. Sed sufficiet ad impetum aquarum propulsandum
aggerem ex fascibus sarmentorum vel cespitibus herbosis ex prato

succisis aut ruinarum excrementis seu etiam truncorum et lapidum transversariis molibus vel, ut Nitocris apud Assyrios fecit, ex concreto limo, quali apud Gallias maxima flumina quasi pensilia videmus compaginare. Cavendum tamen ne si fluminis partem alio avertere vel in fossas vel lacus derivare voluerimus, prius aggeres ex opposito et quodammodo transverso fluvio construantur, quam exploratam habeamus utriusque loci profunditatem et altitudinem, ne nobis quod Artanatri regi contigit evenisse doleamus. Ille enim, vel quod rationem fluminum non haberet vel ut creditur nominis propagandi cupiditate, Melam fluvium qui in Euphratem confluebat, aggeribus ad illius exitum appositis obstruxit, ita morosum et tumidum reddidit, ut totam regionem late inundaret. [Er] Nec multo post, moles illa aggeris interpellata aquis tantis turbinibus tantoque abrupit impetu, ut multa secum arva traxerit multaque ex parte Galatiam Phrygiamque vasta[ve]rit. Hominis insolentiam senatus mulctavit talentis triginta. Idem etiam contigisset Iphicrati Stiphalin obsidenti, cum aquam Erasini fluminis adiectis innumerabilibus spongiis obcludere conatus fuit, ni Iovis monitu revocatus destitisset. Adhibita igitur diligenti et exacta cura hoc primum inundationum incommodum facile praevideri ac resarciri poterit.

Fames

Secundum alluvionis malum est fames et rerum omnium caritas, quod etiam per accidens evenit et per alluvionem duntaxat antequam messes colligantur. Nam, si postquam frumenta horreis condita sunt, id accidat, nihil detrimenti providis affert inundatio nec si afferat illud tale est ut facile ex vicinarum provinciarum frugibus fames ipsa reprimi possit. Ubi igitur hominum consilio et providentia incommodum tolli vel leviter ferri potest, illud ex accidenti contigisse iudicabimus.

Pestilentia

Tertium vero et irreparabile damnum quod inundationes ex sui natura a nobis portendunt, est pestilentia, quae nullis hominum artibus, nullo ingenio emedari potest, nisi placato Deo. Haec cum ex multis causis oriri possit, quas diffusius explicat Ioannes de sancto Nazario in libro *De pestilentia*, tum maxime ex aquis limo commixtis et stagnantibus nasci manifestum est, ut probat Galenus in libro

De differentiis febrium. Qui quidem limus calore obsitus, vapores 79
quosdam loetales et pestilentes emittit, quibus mortalium corda
contagioso anhelitu soporantur et pestilentia afficiuntur, qualem
apud Athenienses evenisse meminet Thucidides, et Illyria pene
tota eodem modo vastata fuit, ut Appianus Alexandrinus auctor
est. Cum igitur inundationes plurimum afferant limi ac omnium
locorum sordes, plura etiam reptilia et cadavera secum trahant, non
est dubitandum quod necessitate quadam cogente vapores debeant
ex ea gigni et emitti quibus humana corpora conficiantur, ut factum
fuisse constat Pelagii tempore. Et credendum est ex eadem etiam
causam provenisse pestilentiam illam saevissimam quam historici
referunt contigisse Leone Sauro imperante, ubi trecenta et eo
civium millia Romae peste consumpta sunt, et plures alia, de quibus
secunda particula diximus. Quod malum ideo Romae facilius gigni
ex praemissa causa poterit, quia limus ille aquis commixtus per antra
et [Ev] subterraneos meatus terrae perque cloacas et cellas occultas,
quae Romae plurimae sunt, dimissus non potest omnia ex parte
mundari aut extemplo desiccari, sed loca ipsa semper humectata
remanent et mucosa situque quodam squallida et faeculenta, ex
qua quidem humectatione aer quo inspiramus, ab illis cavernis
emissus, ita concretus efficitur, ita densus et putridus et spissitudine
quadam nebularum et vaporum crassus et caliginosus, ut quodam
modo superciliis haerens aciem oculorum premat et obtundat ac
loetalem spiritum reddat. Atque propterea Aegypti illi praesertim
qui ad Lybiam spectant, inter alias gentes maxime gloriantur quod 80
ibi nunquam aurae corrumpantur vaporibus nec varientur esseque
ob id valitudine integerrima, ut refert Herodotus.

Nam motu fieri quidem opinor ut surgentes a terra vapores
aut dissipentur aut motibus incalescentibus concoquantur. Aer
enim motu vehementer hilarescit. Nam, sicut aquae ni moveantur
vitium capiunt, ita et aer reclusus situ contabescit et tristissimos
producit exitus, ut auctor est Antonius Guainerius in tractatu
Pestilentiae capitulo I, ubi refert haec expertum fuisse in quibusdam
navibus aquarum. Ac etiam super Ticinensium campania in castro
Nicolini de Becharia, ubi aperientibus puteum veneficus inclusus
aer inde erupens, mortem intulit; et apud Babylonem in templo
Apollonis inventam refert Capitolinus historicus auream arculam
pervetustam, ex qua corruptus et perinde veneficus inclusus aer,

cum illa refringeretur, sese effundens non eos solum interemit, qui tunc prope aderant, verum et contagionibus pestem atrocissimam in totam Asiam usque ad Parthos intulit. Ex Amiano item Marcellino historico legimus M. Antonini et Veri temporibus apud Seleuciam post direptum templum et Romam perlatum simulacrum Comici Apollinis fuisse per milites inventum angustum et prius conclusum ac Chaldaeorum vatibus foramen, quod ubi praedae studio referarunt, pestilens exiluerit vapor tam atrox et tam detestabilis, ut a Persarum finibus intra Galliam usque infecta omnia sint tetro et funesto morbo.

81   Ex praemissis igitur apparet quantum detrimenti afferat aer vapore quodam inclusus, quantum mali inundationum limus ex quo aer ille nebulosus gignitur, sicut etiam de palude quadam exsiccata refert Servius, quae pestilentiam produxit. Nilus etiam qui plus aequo exercuerat et cum luto multa et varia animantia concreta restiterant, quae deinde siccata putruerant, saevam produxit pestem. Et Roma olim porticibus et subgrundis nimium adumbrata, aestatis tempore pestilens erat ut Pomponius et Blondus meminerunt, non alia ra- [E2r] tione nisi propter vapores terrae et Tyberis nebulas angustissimis porticibus reclusas. Quamobrem censuerunt physici ad salutem civitatum pertinere nec nimis angustas vel occupata habere vias, ne recludatur aer densus et humidus, neque rursus nimis latas, ut solis aestu torreantur. Nam, ut scribit Cornelius Tacitus, Nero vias urbis dilataverat et ex eo facta fuit minus salubris propter solis aestum, qui eam fervidiorem reddiderat.

Medium igitur servabitur ne magna latitudine priventur umbra neque nimium angusta sit, ut aer computrescat, ut facile Romae contigit. Nam Petrus Vergerius in libro *De situ veteris Romae* testatur urbes quas aut violentus casus destruxit aut vetustas exedit, esse aere insalubres, cum per ruinam plures concavitates et subterranea loca sint occlusa et parum salubrem emittant aerem. In quo genere ponit Romam, Aquileiam, Ravennam, Senogalliam, Adriam et pleraque alias vetustissimas urbes temporum iniuriam collapsas.

82   Nam nihil magis naturae hominum offici quam aer humidus, cuius ratione Austrum affirmant physici prae coeteris hominibus esse noxium etiam animantibus brutis; nam Austro flante non sine periculo esse in pascuis animalia volunt neque ciconias temere se

austris committere, delphines etiam per Aquilonem voces audire, Austro vero tardius et non nisi ex adverso redditas. Anguillas item Aquilone stante flante sine aquis senos durare dies afferunt, Austro non durare. Tantamque inesse huic vento propter eius densitatem et crassitudinem, in morbos vim, ut eum vitae corrosivum appellent.

Putant enim humidis tabescere corpora omnia, siccis autem vel calidis reparari. Et propterea Appianus scripsit Numidas ea de re maxime longaevos esse, quod hyemem nequicquam habeant. Sive igitur huiusmodi aeris humiditas causetur ex regionis situ sive ex cloacarum immundiciis, quae, ut volunt iurisconsulti titulo *De cloacis*, coelum pestilens reddunt et aedificiorum ruinam minantur, nisi mundentur, sive etiam ex limo inundationibus invecto, satis apparet hoc esse malum ex naturali quadam ipsius rei proprietate procedens ac humana providentia inevitabile.

Acerbius tamen illud est quod ab inundationibus procedit. Nam cum limus aqua commixtus occupet loca subterranea et latentes concavitates urbis mundari non possint, aer redditur infectus, non sic in cloacis et aquarum ductibus, quae arte mundari possunt et multum civitatibus conferunt, si purgentur. Nam sicuti ad salubritatem civitatum pertinet habere ductus et cloacas bene mundatas, ita ad insalubritatem refertur eas habere immundas ob praemissam causam, vel nullas habere ad quas sordes domus quae aerem densum reddunt, deriventur et decurrant. Propterea Smyrnam [E2v] urbem, in qua Dolobella Trebonium obsidione liberavit, dicunt historici inter alias urbes fuisse pulcherrimam viarum directionem et operum ornamentis, sed alioqui sordidam et pestilentem quae cloacae non sint, quibus immundiciae et sordes emissae excipiantur, qua de causa foeditate hospites offendebat. Idem de Sena Ethruriae civitate nobilissima fert, quod solum ad ornamentum et commodum civitatis desunt cloacae. Ex quo fit ut, non solum prima ultimaque noctis vigilia, quibus horis congestarum sordium vasa ex fenestris funduntur, tota foeteat, verum et inde interdum obscoena et graviter humectata sit, quod cum nos ipsi aliquando experti simus, ita etiam de hac re auctor est Albertus libro I *De architectura*.

Ex his igitur satis constat quantum mali, quantum etiam damni afferat limus immundissimus inundationum aquis undique collectus et mixtus qui, ut saepe dictum est, per obtrusa urbis loca dimissus

83

perque antra cloacas et meatus reclusus necessaria quadam ratione pestilentiam gignit, ut saepe fecit et secunda particula tractatus enarravimus.

Quae omnia cum in manu Dei Optimi Maximi sint posita neque hominum consilio evitari valeant, eundem pia mente rogabimus, dignetur eam finibus nostris averteret et tandem iam laborum tantorum misereri.

84

Finis

Romae apud F. Minitium Calvum

Anno MDXXXI

❧ ❧

❧

DOCUMENTARY APPENDIX: CONTEMPORARY REPORTS ON THE FLOOD OF 1530

A. Anonymous of Bologna, *Diluvio di Roma* of 1530

B. Benvenuto Cellini, Extract from his *Autobiography*

C. Giovanni Domenico Sanga, Letter to Duke Alessandro de' Medici

D. Excerpt from the Journal of Cardinal Jerome Aléandre

E. Letters from the *Diary* of Marino Sanuto

☫

A.

Anonymous, Diluvio di Roma che fu a VII d'ottobre, l'anno MDXXX... con ordinata discrittione di parte in parte, *Benvenuto Gasparoni, ed., in* Arti e Lettere: Scritti Raccolti da Francesco e Benvenuto Gasparoni, 2 vols. (*Rome: Tipografia delle Scienze Matematiche e Fisiche, 1865*), 2:81–98, 106–31; *text at 87–91.*

The anonymous work published here is found in a small, quarto-sized gathering found in a larger volume of 426 pages, which contains 102 miscellaneous works. It was printed in Bologna by Giovanni Battista di Phaelli in November 1530, that is, immediately after the flood. Although the work was of seemingly limited circulation, the Florentine historian Marco Guazzo (1496–1556) read it and copied parts of the text verbatim into his *Historie di M. Marco Guazzo di tutti i fatti degni di memoria nel mondo* published initially in 1540.

⚛

[87] I can hardly believe that there is anyone anywhere in the world so devoid of piety that, upon learning of even a thousandth part of the destruction — no, the annihilation — of vanquished Rome, an abundant fountain of tears would not pour from his eyes, unless he were made completely of stone or had been raised in the forest on the milk of the most savage beast. I know well that you shall receive from me a letter [written] more with tears than ink. I call upon my bitter pain that does not want to contend with me over my words of lament, and I summon the kindness of the gods to my aid so that they will be present to respond to the sound of sadness, to voices full of bitterness, to this pen full of pain. For by narrating only a small part of the ruin of this wretched city, I hope to provoke pity in the eyes not only of those now alive but also of those who shall be born here for the next thousand years. If someone wanted to describe fully the entire event, it would be necessary to compose a long poem, and I am not sure whether even such a strong wit would not begin to waver even at the outset and, worn out, would not even have the strength to retreat from so demanding an undertaking, since it involves so much material that it would not be possible to contain it all in a small

volume. But why do I linger so much in the preface and not come immediately to this terrifying narration of such a horrible event!

I shall not fail to inform you that before this flood many prodigies were seen. From these a prediction was made that some strange and terrible event would be seen in this unfortunate city. A monster was born that did not have feet, hands, face, eye, or nose so that one was unable even to guess what it resembled, and it looked neither like a male or female, and had the appearance of neither man nor beast. In addition to this, many signs in the air were seen day and night that created much wonder and fear, and some saw the sun [rise] before daybreak for less than an hour and then sink into the east and not appear until the regular time.

[88] Two months before this flood, a nun of outstanding devotion and sanctity, a model of religious life, a mirror of chastity, an example of virtue, a woman illuminated by a prophetic spirit loosed her tongue like the wisest Sybil in the following words: "The entire moon of September shall not pass before Rome shall be oppressed by misfortune more severe than there was at the time of the Sack." But in our times little or no faith is given to the words of just and religious persons, and who would have been so observant as to consider such a possibility? Rome was already so much in the process of rebuilding that one no longer remembered the Bourbon.[1] The whole world was at peace, and who but God would have been led to believe that such ruin — something so far beyond human imagining — would suddenly appear in the midst of human happiness?

On the third of October, which was a Monday, His Holiness our lord left Rome to go to Ostia to relax a bit with the intention of staying there three or four days. But His Blessedness was not there long before he regretted that he had left because he had a quite difficult and uncomfortable stay there.

On Tuesday, which was the fourth of October, and on Wednesday the weather was bright and serene. On Thursday, which was the sixth, it began to rain so unendingly that it seemed that all the floodgates of

---

1. "The Bourbon" refers to Charles III, duke of Bourbon (1490–1527) who was killed in the initial attack on Rome in the Sack of 1527, and is a way of referring to the Sack. See pp. 7–8 n. 8.

heaven had been opened. For two days and nights continuous rain resulted in an overwhelming flood that brought about a wondrous transformation in the lakes, rivers, torrents, rivulets, ponds, springs, and marshes. In addition to the fact that it became full enough beyond any measure to form a lake by itself, the proud Tiber, that most swift of rivers, was increased by [the waters of] the Lago di Piediluco.[2]

Consequently, all or almost all of the aqueducts were unable to handle the raging force and universal abundance of the water that they were receiving from the aforesaid lake. They burst and joined the Tiber. This great mass of water, all gathered together, flowed into the sea so that its supply was far greater than usual. It was a wondrous thing that at that time the sea was at high tide (it rises and falls every six hours). In addition to the fact that the sea was beating upon the shore, the wind was very strong at that time in the direction of the waves. Upon reaching the mouth, therefore, the head of the river swell could not gain access to the sea nor break through the waves that were kept high by the wind and by their natural motion [when they strike the shore]. Unable to flow out, [the river] therefore began to swell and to spread widely through fields and meadows. In an instant, dry land there became a wide sea and, where previously one had drawn a plow with oxen and cast seed, one could quite safely traverse in good boats.

On Friday, which was the seventh, at 8:00 at night, the water began to spread through the city and massively increased. The underground structures, of which there is an infinite number intended for the storage of wine and wood, were filled with water in an instant. Then the streets and rooms at ground level began to flood. Infinite numbers [of people] were caught asleep, and truly they all slept an eternal sleep and will rise on the Judgment Day. Some fled to upper rooms, some to rooftops. On Saturday morning, some withdrew to certain large buildings that they thought should be safe because of their height. Others [retreated] to higher ground [89], such as hills, meadows, and vineyards, and each person took care only for their own safety. Without distinction, people — some on foot, some on horseback — searched for a place to save themselves from such

2.   This lake is situated along the border between Umbria and Lazio, a few miles south-east of the city of Terni.

horrendously raging waters. Fathers did not wait for sons, sons did not care for fathers, brothers did not [look after] brothers, nor did friends think about how to save anyone other than themselves.

What a thing worthy of compassion it was to hear those laments, the cries, the strident voices, the shouts, the sobs, the clapping, the tearing of clothes, the scratching of faces, the beating of chests that filled the air! A more wretched situation was never known. These are extraordinary times when one sees poor children being carried away by the waves right in front of their sweetest mothers who are unable to extend a lifeline to them but instead await a similar end in death. Others saw a father, a mother, a husband, brothers, sisters, a wife, friends being carried off to a similar fate. No one knew how to or had the strength to rescue anyone, even themselves. The water continued rising for twenty-four hours from Friday night at 8:00 until Saturday night at 8:00. It began to rise so much that it overcame even the tallest buildings and the great towers, and so it ruined the plans of many who fled to such places, which were then flooded. Others were washed away by the water along with houses torn from their foundations and met their miserable end that way. In the end, the only places spared by such raging [water] were Monte Giordano, where there were about a thousand horses; Sant'Agostino;[3] the house of Baroccio di Farnese[4] (though the storerooms were filled with water because they were underground); Trastevere from the main street up so that the storehouses of [the port of] Ripa were safe. All the rest of Rome went under. Others who had taken refuge on top of very high buildings and towers, then descended by rope and lowered themselves down. Where once people traveled on foot or on horseback, there were [now] boats going from neighborhood to neighborhood through all of Rome to bring food supplies.

The water flowed with so much force that it ruined the cobbled streets and created a channel so wide as to pass into the moat of Castel [Sant'Angelo]. Rather than flowing out, it has cut through both abutments of Ponte Sant'Angelo,[5] which were massive and [made of] marble. Had the raging waters lasted a bit longer, the entire bridge

---

3. The church of Sant'Agostino is near Piazza Navona.

4. We have not been able to identify this person.

5. For Ponte Sant'Angelo see pp. 45–47 and n. 92.

would certainly have been destroyed. The Ponte Sisto broke again,[6] as did the Ponte Quattro Capi.[7] Dead animals like horses, mules, oxen, asses, and the like were innumerable. Even worse, among men and women of different ages at least 3,000 were drowned.

These supplies were lost: baked bread, oil, flour, bolts of wool, bolts of silk, brocades, tapestries,[8] bolts of linen, and every sort of household goods to the value of one million in gold. This does not include the grain, which amounted to 150,000 rubbi[9] and four ships at the [port of] Ripa loaded with grain that sank with many men on board, and the 30,000 barrels of wine, [that were destroyed] according to a report made to our lord [the pope]. It also does not account for the ruined buildings nor the buildings about to collapse, which are innumerable, nor does this include the damage to sown fields and the other fruit-bearing trees that were destroyed. The mills for grinding grain were all ruined. More than 400 buildings — from public halls[10] to houses — were leveled by the incredible swift current of the rains that were falling, especially those located along the bank of the river on both sides, [90] especially [the houses] of the Banchieri,[11] [those] to

---

6.   See pp. 47–48 n. 95.

7.   I.e., Ponte Fabricio. This ancient bridge, which is still standing, was built in 62 BCE and linked the Tiber Island to the Campus Martius, near the Theater of Marcellus. It was restored in 1679 by Pope Innocent XI. See Jean-Marie Salamito, "Pons Fabricius," LTUR 4:109–10.

8.   *Panni di razza*, i.e., *arazzi* (tapestries).

9.   Spelled *"ruggi"* in the text. In sixteenth-century Rome a *rubbio* was a weight amount of grain: 1 *rubbio* = 640 *libbre*. The total loss in present-day tonnage would be c.35,900 tons. Given that the average grain capacity of a modern grain barge is 1500 tons, the loss of grain would have equaled the load of 24 grain barges. The loss, therefore, was probably equal to all of the grain stores in the city, since the grain warehouses would probably have been next to the river, as in Roman times. To avoid such a fate, the ancient Romans designed their granaries (*horrea*) specially to resist flooding. For ancient warehouses, see Aldrete, *Floods*, 134–36 and 138–41.

10.   Here we interpret the author's word *"teatri"* in the generic sense of halls for public assemblies and performances.

11.   Banchi.

the right of the Altoviti Fiorentini,[12] [those] of the via di San Rocco,[13] [those of] the Strada del Popolo,[14] [that of] Chigi[15] on via Giulia,[16] and various other places.

On the tenth day of the month, which was a Monday, around thirty houses were destroyed on via Giulia, and that evening, at three in the morning, there was destroyed on that same via Giulia the palace of Signor Eusebio, former master of the house of the most reverend [cardinal] of San Giorgio, which cost around 10,000 ducats. It collapsed upon Signor Eusebio, who was the head of the house. In that same place about forty members of his household died. Signor Eusebio was generally believed to have had 30,000 ducats in cash in the bank; in his offices more than 10,000.

It was a great miracle that two children of two years old, clinging to each other, were carried away by the water on their coarse-cloth mattress. They were pulled to the riverbank safe and sound and without the slightest injury. And these toddlers are [now] staying with Signor Guido de' Medici who takes care of them as if they were his own children.

On Saturday, which was the eighth of the month, His Holiness our lord had just had lunch when, because the flooding river had

---

12. The Lungotevere degli Altoviti and Lungotevere dei Fiorentini are located just south of Ponte Sant'Angelo, on the left bank of the Tiber.

13. The church of San Rocco and the modern Largo San Rocco are on the left bank, next to the Mausoleum of Augustus and the Ara Pacis.

14. Via di Ripetta, which was previously called via Leonina. On the construction of this street between 1517 and 1520, see Carmen Genovese and Daniela Sinisi, Pro ornatu et publica utilitate: L'attività della Congregazione cardinalizia super viis, pontibus et fontibus nella Roma di fine '500 (Rome: Gangemi Editore, 2010), xlii n. 83.

15. The street leading to the palace of Agostino Chigi, i.e., the Villa della Farnesina. For the villa, see p. 68 n. 154.

16. This name is spelled "Tullia" in the text, a misspelling of via Giulia, on which there were several buildings that collapsed during this flood. One of them was the palace of Signor Eusebio, which is mentioned below and, according to Gómez (p. 70 n. 155) and Sanga (Appendix C, pp. 133–35.), was on via Giulia.

closed off every way of entry and exit, he decided to return to Rome because in Ostia there were no supplies even for dinner. There truly was most prudent planning in this because every moment longer he stayed there, His Holiness remained at risk of being harmed by the water's violence. He came back to Rome, with water constantly over the bellies of the horses, at the greatest risk to himself and to his entire court. Once he arrived in Rome and wished to go to [his] palace,[17] all four bridges — [which are] of wondrous height — were covered by water, i.e., Ponte Sant'Angelo, Ponte Sta. Maria, Ponte Sisto, and Ponte Quattro Capi. When he could not proceed further (since he would have needed a large boat), he turned around and headed to Monte Cavallo[18] to stay at Sant'Agata [dei Goti], which is the titular church of the Very Reverend Cardinal Ridolfi, his nephew.[19] He stayed there until Monday evening.

On the [church of Sta. Maria sopra] Minerva there are markers placed where the Tiber has spread and flooded on other occasions. The biggest marker and flood were at the time of Pope Alexander [VI]. Now the Tiber has surpassed the higher mark by two *canne*.[20] At the time of Alexander many places were preserved [from the flood] but now very few.

In the Borgo the water was higher than a pike;[21] in the Agone[22] there was a very great amount of water; in the Rotonda,[23] one saw a sea; almost all the altars and oratories have been ruined. The churches

---

17. The Vatican Palace.

18. The Quirinale. So named after the *cavalli*, the horses of the ancient statue of the Dioscuri still there.

19. Niccolò Ridolfi (1501–50). For his career, see Lucinda Byatt, "Ridolfi, Niccolò," DBI 87 (2016): 471–75; and Salvador Miranda, "Ridolfi, Niccolò," in *The Cardinals of the Holy Roman Church*, https://cardinals.fiu.edu/bios1517-ii.htm#Ridolfi.

20. One *canna* equals to 7.15 feet (or 2.2 meters). See Figure 7.

21. The Borgo Pio, which is also known as the Città Leonina, the neighborhood around St. Peter's. The pike (*pica*) is used here as a generic term that refers to a length taller than a man.

22. Piazza Navona.

23. Sta. Maria della Rotonda (the Pantheon).

are full of mud, and the ground has raised the floor of the church by a pace.[24] There is no one now who would have judged that there would have been churches that truly seem like abandoned and derelict caves.

It remains only to say that God alone knows when the underground cellars shall be empty. [They are now] full of water and of that filth that gives off the great stench that produces a deadly plague. In the end, in part because of wars, in part because of the plague in times past, and in part because of the present flood, an infinite number of people have died or left [the city]. But we cannot expect new [people] to come here, since there is nothing to give them to eat. His Holiness our lord along with his entire court was therefore compelled to leave; and the disconsolate, sorrowful city remains alone. This [city] that was the queen of all others in former times [is] now besieged by great misery within, and she is not able to give comfort anymore. [91] And so one hopes that heavenly piety shall take care of it and the wisdom of our Lord shall not allow it to become a den of ravenous beasts [i.e., thieves and other criminals].

This incomparable destruction saw more serious damage, and Rome suffered more during the four days of this accursed event than it did when the most cruel army of the Bourbon put everything to fire and sword on May 27, 1527. For so many months [Rome] was pillaged by the nations of the Bourbon, enemies of Latin blood! O devastated city, that you were beset with such a great calamity so quickly! First, you are afflicted by famine, then deprived by plague of such a numerous and beautiful people. You have been almost burned and destroyed by a humiliating sack, so many people have died a violent death; so many monasteries of most holy women dedicated to Christ became shameful and despised places. Gold, silver, the most precious vestments dedicated to divine worship and to preserve the most holy remains of the blessed bodies [of the saints] have been stolen and put to the worst possible use.[25] Now, sooner than one could expect, [you are] almost drowned in water, when there was no consideration for age, gender, social class, or

---

24. About a foot.

25. The author here refers to both vestments worn by clergy and vestments and fabrics that adorned the bodies of interred saints.

quality. It would be very inhumane if someone were to keep a dry face when reading about your wretched fate.

Printed in Bologna, in the month of November 1530, by Giovanni Battista di Phaelli.

⚌ ⚌

B.

Benvenuto Cellini, Vita di Benvenuto Cellini, *Orazio Bacci, ed. (Florence: Sansoni, 1901), 111.*

Benvenuto Cellini (1500–1571) was a Florentine artist best known for his skills as a goldsmith and sculptor.[26] He worked in Rome intermittently and wrote a famous autobiography, of which this is an excerpt.

⚌

As I was about to finish my work, there occurred that massive flood that filled all of Rome with water. I was seeing what [the flood] was doing when it was already late in the day. [The bells] were already sounding 10:00 o'clock and the waters were increasing in an extraordinary way. Because my house and workshop faced [via dei] Banchi[27] on the front, and its back was several *braccia*[28] higher since it faced Monte Giordano,[29]

---

26.   See Angela Biancofiore, *Benvenuto Cellini artiste-écrivain: L'homme à l'oeuvre* (Paris: Harmattan, 1998); Ettore Camesasca and Nino Borsellino, "Cellini, Benvenuto," DBI 23 (1979): 440–51; Margaret A. Gallucci, *Benvenuto Cellini: Sexuality, Masculinity, and Artistic Identity in the Renaissance* (New York: Palgrave Macmillan, 2003); and Margaret A. Gallucci and Paolo L. Rossi, ed., *Benvenuto Cellini: Sculptor, Goldsmith, Writer* (New York: Cambridge University Press, 2004).

27.   A plaque commemorating Benvenuto Cellini's workshop can be seen on the front side of the palace in Largo Tassoni 319.

28.   The *braccio* (arm) is a unit of measurement that corresponds to variable lengths depending on the city. Here Cellini is probably using the Florentine *braccio*, which is equivalent to 58.32 centimeters (c.23 inches).

29.   This hill, which gives the name to the modern street (via di Monte Giordano), is bounded by via dei Coronari, vicolo Domizio, and via della Vetrina.

I thought first to save my life, then to save my honor. I took with me all my valuable things and left my gold work to my workers on guard. So, without shoes, I descended quickly through my windows and waded through those waters as best I could so that I made it all the way to Monte Cavallo,[30] where I found Signor Giovanni Gaddi, cleric of the [Apostolic] Camera, and Bastiano, the Venetian painter.[31] I approached Signor Giovanni and gave him all those valuable things, [asking him] to keep them for me. He treated me as if I were his own brother. Then, after a few days, the fury of the waters passed and I returned to my workshop and finished the work with such good fortune, thanks to God's grace and my own great efforts, that it was held to be the most beautiful work that was ever seen in Rome.

≋ ≋

C.

Excerpt from a Letter of Giovanni Battista Sanga to Duke Alessandro de' Medici (October 15, 1530), translated from Lettere di Principi le quali si scrivono o ai principi o ragionano di principi, *3 vols. (Venice: Giordano Zirletti, 1577), 3:114r–15r.*

Giovanni Battista Sanga (1496–1532) was a humanist literary figure and secretary to cardinals and popes. He served as a Florentine ambassador and influential advisor in Rome from 1524 to 1525 and then intermittently until his death in 1532. He was there at the time of the flood. His letter is addressed to Alessandro de' Medici (1510–37), who would rule Florence from 1531 until his death.[32]

≋

[114v] Also we have had here an unheard-of deluge. The Tiber has risen so much that it has gone throughout Rome, and the water in certain places has risen eight palms higher than it reached in the time of [Pope] Alexander [VI], which was considered the greatest

---

30. The Quirinale. See p. 130 n. 18.

31. Sebastiano del Piombo (c.1485–1547).

32. See Marcello Simonetta, "Sanga, Giovan Battista," DBI 90 (2017): 182–83.

of floods at the time. Boats went all the way to Piazza SS. Apostoli,[33] and on this side[34] the water reached the steps of St. Peter's. Our lord [pope], returning from Ostia, where he had gone for the air on the 4th [of the month], spent two days at Sant'Agata on Monte Cavallo[35] because he was unable to make his way to his palace, when we were all besieged [by water] in our houses.

The damage has been so massive to an afflicted and exhausted city like this one that it seemed to be another sack. The new wine has been lost, as has been a great amount of the old, along with so much grain that in an instant the price quadrupled. Without help from Sicily, we cannot imagine surviving here this year. Fodder, hay, wood have been almost all lost, and infinite goods have been ruined because the flooding was so sudden that nothing could be saved. [The flood] carried away animals and many people who found themselves either in low-lying areas or houses that were surrounded by the waters before they could save themselves.

The river left its bed this past Friday, which was the 7th, and it rose all Saturday until 9:00 in the evening; and all of Sunday it was impossible to manage Rome without a boat. On Monday, [the Tiber] returned to its bed. It left the streets and the houses so damaged that it is terrifying to go through Rome. Yet, although the waters have receded, every day the ruin caused by this deluge continues. In different places in Rome many structurally weakened houses have been destroyed, and many large ones are propped up since the water undermined their foundations. The entire bank where the boats docked in Trastevere is gone.[36] On the via Giulia behind the Banchi[37] your Excellency knows how beautiful the houses were. There are obvious signs that few of them will survive.

---

33.   Piazza SS. Apostoli is located behind via del Corso, near Piazza Venezia.

34.   The right bank of the Tiber.

35.   Piazza del Quirinale. See p. 130 n. 18.

36.   The Porto di Ripa.

37.   Via dei Banchi Vecchi is a street parallel to via Giulia farther from the Tiber.

The following event struck the greatest fear into the entire city. The great house belonging to M. Eusebio (a rich courtier who was formerly servant of the cardinal of San Giorgio³⁸ and considered to be very respectable) collapsed on Sunday evening at 3:00 in the morning while he was in the house with about thirty other people, because the river had removed the ground underneath. All the people and animals staying there were killed. The way it collapsed is even more frightening because the house did not fall on just one side but sank all at once, as if it fell into a ditch.

I would give your Excellency too much [115r] to read if I recounted all the damage from this flood. The event would have frightened the city even more (believing that the flood signified some greater evil), if it had not learned that in many other places the waters did tremendous damage. In Viterbo, which is located on high ground, as your Excellency knows, the waters from the rains carried away a large part of the wall. It is said that in the regions of Ferrara and Mantua, they have had infinite damage, and in that area we learned of the same flooding from the letter of the Monsignor of Vasona.³⁹

From Rome

October 13, 1530.

꙲ ꙲

D.

Henri Omont, ed., "Journal autobiographique du cardinal Jérôme Aléandre (1480–1530) publié d'après manuscrits de Paris et d'Udine," Notices et extraits des manuscrits de la Bibliothèque Nationale et d'autres bibliothèques 35 (1895): 2–115, at 98.

Born near Treviso in 1480, Girolamo Aleandro distinguished himself for his learning and taught Greek at the University of Paris

---

38. Possibly Girolamo Grimaldi, who was installed as cardinal deacon of San Giorgio in Velabro in 1528. See Salvador Miranda, "Grimaldi, Girolamo (?–1543)," in *Cardinals of the Holy Roman Church*, https://cardinals.fiu.edu/bios1527-ii.htm#Grimaldi.

39. The remainder of the letter deals with other matters unrelated to the flood.

for a time. In 1519, while on an embassy to Rome, he was made papal librarian by Pope Leo X. Aleandro was soon sent as a papal envoy to German lands and was one of the chief opponents of Martin Luther. Pope Clement VII appointed him archbishop of Brindisi, and in the 1530s he was made a cardinal *in pectore*. He died in 1542.[40]

❧

Sunday, October 23, 1530, at 11:00 PM. Letters by Domenico Mussi [came] from the city about the flooding of the city and the almost universal destruction in that city.[41] ...From the letters that I received today and yesterday, I see that there was a flood of the Tiber greater than any in the memory of our fathers. Not only are all the wine cellars full [of water] just like all the [other] underground [rooms], but also there has been no house safe from this flood except those on the hills. More than 300 houses have been destroyed; many more would already have fallen were they not propped up with beams. The water everywhere was reaching the second floor. We should be afraid of the plague, for in a similar situation in this same month, in the time of Emperor Maurice and Pope Pelagius (whom Gregory the Great succeeded) the Tiber flooded, and there followed that most savage of all plagues that killed Pelagius as well. After Gregory succeeded him, after killing almost everyone, it was only just extinguished in the end through the septiform litany that Gregory instituted. On this, see [John] the Deacon and others. The same thing was happening at that time in areas of Venice and Liguria, especially in the city of Verona. [Flooding] destroyed a good part of this city's walls to the foundations, and the water rose all the way up to the upper windows of the church of San Zeno; but it did not enter, as Lord Gregory testifies.[42]

❧ ❧

---

40.   In addition to the information in the edition cited, see Giuseppe Alberigo, "Aleandro, Girolamo," DBI 2 (1960): 129–35; and Salvador Miranda, "Aleandro, Girolamo (1480–1542)," in *The Cardinals of the Holy Roman Church*, https://cardinals.fiu.edu/bios1536.htm#Aleandro.

41.   The first sections of the journal entry deal with other matters.

42.   See Gómez's account of the Fourteenth Flood, pp. 51–53 above.

E.

Marino Sanuto, I Diarii di Marino Sanuto 54, Guglielmo Berchet, Nicolò Barozzi, and Marco Allegri, ed. (Venice: Fratelli Visentini, 1899), cols. 73–76.

Marino Sanuto (or Sanudo) the Younger (1466–1536) was born into a patrician Venetian family and was active in various capacities in the Venetian government during most of his adult life. From the age of fifteen he reported in detail on all of his own activities and much else. His voluminous writings, including his diaries, are an essential source for the history of Venice and for other locations as well.[43] Here he reproduces three letters that describe the Tiber River flood.

🔊

From Rome there then came at the ninth hour on the 18th [of October] another courier with a letter from our orator. It describes conversations held with the pope and about that flood of the Tiber. The most serious damage has been done, and [the flood] has ruined more than 100 houses. Fodder has been carried away along with the new wines, so that horse fodder has gone up 50%, what cost 3 ducats/*rubbio* now costs 5,[44] which is worth 2 of our [ducats] per bushel.[45]

🔊

Copy of letter of Ser Antonio Surian, doctor and cavaliere, orator at Rome, given on October 15, 1530, written to Ser Agustin Surian, his brother.[46]

---

43. Matteo Melchiorre, "Sanudo, Marino il Giovane," DBI 90 (2017): 498–504.

44. Spelled *"rugio"* in the text. See p. 128 n. 9.

45. The term *"staro"* is an alternate spelling of *"staio"* from the Latin *sextarius*. It means "bushel."

46. The brothers Antonio Surian (1480/83–1542) and Agustin Surian (dates unknown), were from a Venetian patriciate family. Their uncle, Antonio Surian (1451–1508) was the patriarch of Venice from 1504 until his death in 1508. The younger Antonio received a doctorate from the University of Padua and then began a public career as a diplomat and

On the 7th of the present [month], on account of the extremely heavy and constant rains (as well as the eclipse of the moon), the Tiber rose for more than forty hours. The flood of that river was of such violence and abundance that it surpassed every ancient flood by almost three *braccia*, and especially [the flood] that happened in the time of Alexander VI of happy memory. It ruined the whole of this wretched city. It provokes great compassion to see people wandering the streets in shock. The [flood] broke the large parapet of the Ponte Sant'Angelo. The cobbled streets were stripped of stones; a world of buildings was destroyed; many people drowned; all the mills were broken and carried away. All the fodder, which in Rome they usually store in underground rooms, was destroyed. The new wine, which had just been placed in cellars, was ruined; and a world's worth of horses and animals was drowned. In the house of the most reverend Grimani,[47] where I was staying initially, the water reached the first floor, so that the Lord God helped me realize that I needed to leave from there to go to where I am staying now, which is a high place. I did not go there deprived of possessions, although the water took from me twelve barrels of new wine that I had placed in my cellar. My grain, soaked and destroyed, is now worthless, as is also the barley, the spelt, and the oats. In short, I was despoiled of all the provisions that I had made for the coming year. This damage will cost me 500 ducats, but may God be thanked for all.

If the matter had simply ended there, it could have been remedied. But day after day, one hears about buildings collapsing and killing their inhabitants. Both houses that had taken on water and those that had not, fall in this way. But now, if I — or even the cardinals — want to go to the [Vatican] palace, it is easier to go around the area and to take a detour three times longer to avoid going through areas at such risk of falling buildings. Just this morning, I wanted to

---

ambassador. In 1529, he was appointed ambassador to Pope Clement VII, and in April of 1530 he was in Rome and remained there until May 1531. See Giuseppe Trebbi, "Surian, Antonio," DBI 94 (2019): 541–44, where Agustin is mentioned as one of his four siblings (three brothers and one sister).

47. On Venetian Cardinal Marino Grimani (1489–1545), see Giampiero Brunelli, "Grimani, Marino," DBI 59 (2002): 640–46.

return inside because of the rains, but a building collapsed just in front of me, in which five people died. I felt very sorry for them. In conclusion, we can affirm that the damage to this unfortunate city is extremely great, and no less than was the Sack.

꽃

Copy of letter of Lord Alvise Lippomano from Rome, dated October 14, to Ser Tommaso, his brother.[48]

You ought to have heard about the flood that happened here on the eighth of the month, which has destroyed this entire land. It flowed through the Banchi to the height of a pike; and neither bread nor anything else was found. We have never seen a more horrible sight. Innumerable buildings are destroyed because their cellars are full of water. Among others, three palaces on via Giulia collapsed and, in general, all the buildings show cracks and are being propped up. Everyone flees to the hills and are very afraid. The water has broken the abutments of the Ponte Sant'Angelo and stripped the streets of bricks. Innumerable people have died as well as countless horses and donkeys. The mills are broken; and in short, everything [is] upside down, so that they conclude that it was another Sack. All the grain and wine are lost, and there is a great scarcity of everything. For five days, we have lived on semolina bread. But this is the most terrifying sight: the Agone,[49] the Rotonda,[50] and the Campo de' Fiori seem like the Adriatic Sea, and the

---

48.   Alvise (Luigi) Lippomano (1496–1559) was the natural-born son of a Venetian banker, Bartolomeo Lippomano. He studied in Padua and Rome and was in Rome in the summer of 1522, where he began an ecclesiastic career. In 1528, he was in Orvieto for six months in the court of Clement VII, who had fled there during the Sack. In 1529, he was appointed apostolic *protonotario*. He was in Rome during the flood of 1530 and wrote to his brother Tommaso describing it. See Alexander Koller, "Lippomano, Luigi (Aloisio, Alvise)," DBI 65 (2005): 243–46; and for his later work as a bishop, Giuseppe Alberigo, *I vescovi italiani al Concilio di Trento, 1545–1547* (Florence: G. C. Sansoni [1959]), esp. 73–77 and 84–89; and Oliver Logan, *The Venetian Upper Clergy in the 16th and Early 17th Centuries: A Study in Religious Culture*, 2 vols. (Salzburg: Institut für Anglistik und Amerikanistik, Universität Salzburg, 1995), 1:184–205.

49.   Piazza Navona.

50.   Sta. Maria della Rotonda (the Pantheon).

water has spread so widely through all of Rome that it has reached the steps of the Capitoline, something unheard of before.

✺

Rome, October 10, 1530

To the Lord Duke of Mantua[51]

After I had written my other news to your Excellency, on the seventh of this [month], here in Rome we suffered great pain, distress, and chaos because of an extraordinary flood of the Tiber, which spread throughout the city so that it rose two *braccia*[52] above the height of the [previous flood] marker. There is no memory that something like this had happened for many and many years, and it would be considered almost impossible, if not miraculous, if we had not seen it. On Saturday [the eighth] — not the day before, [which was] the seventh — at sunrise, the water started to reach the Strada del Popolo,[53] and it continued with so much fury that before night came it flooded all of Rome.[54] It continued rising until after 8:00 at night. If the weather had not been good — for many days before it had rained endlessly and only that day, luckily, it did not — everyone would have certainly feared that by God's will this city had to sink and fall into the abyss. For we saw such a great deluge coming with such great force that there was no house in the city that had not at least four or five *braccia*[55] of water up its walls above the ground level, which was horrible and extremely frightening to see.

Still, thank God, at 9:00 the water started to lower, and between yesterday and last night it decreased so much that most of the

---

51.   This refers to Federico II Gonzaga (1500–1540), who became duke of Mantua in 1530. See Gino Benzoni, "Federico II Gonzaga, duca di Mantova e marchese del Monferrato," DBI 45 (1995): 710–22.

52.   About 4 feet.

53.   Via di Ripetta (via Leonina).

54.   Sources agree that the flood lasted 24 hours, from Friday the seventh, at 8:00 at night, up to Saturday the eighth, at 8:00 at night. Here the author is describing what happened on Saturday morning in the area of via di Ripetta.

55.   About 8–10 feet.

streets are clear. But it is a pity to see the state of the houses and streets, full of mud and other filth, which ruined everything. Your Excellency must know that the damage and ruin following this event is so great that it is thought to be little less than that of the Sack.[56] Grain and fodder for horses, which were [stored] in the lower floors of the houses in abundance, are lost. The wines almost all spilled out of their barrels, most of all the local wines, which cannot be kept sealed because of fermentation.[57] All the hay has been ruined, innumerable other goods [are] spoiled and lost, for there was no time or way to save them. Many people died who could not be saved because those poor folks found themselves outside their little houses (which are common here around Rome), so that when the water rose so abruptly and so furiously, they could not do anything other than retreat to their rooftops. There, they cried for mercy and help but in vain. For there was no means to help them, since only two small boats appeared during this flood: one in Rome, the other outside of it. It is easy to imagine what [little] they were able to accomplish amidst such great need.

This event, in addition to bringing incredible damage to all of Rome, is also prompting great fear in everyone's mind because it is both extraordinary and a harbinger of terrible effects. At the very least, a plague is expected, since the ancient Romans observed that the Tiber never flooded without a plague following. And if it comes, God forbid, it will be the complete ruin of this poor city.

Our lord [pope] left Ostia this morning to come back here, thrown out — we might say — by the rain, by the flood, and by hunger, since there was nothing to eat there. But, when His Holiness reached Rome and heard the news, he stopped at Sant'Agata [dei Goti], which is a place near Monte Cavallo,[58] and there he stayed yesterday and today until 9:00 at night. Then, his Blessedness went to his palace[59] but was not very consoled because he saw the wretched scene of ruined houses and workshops, as well as [the ruined] abutments

56. The Sack of Rome in 1527.

57. *Romaneschi*, that is, wines being produced in Rome itself and in the process of fermentation.

58. The Quirinale. See p. 130 n. 18.

59. The Vatican Palace.

of all the bridges that cross the river. In addition to other problems and damage, a great shortage of all supplies is expected. Before this event occurred, all prices were high. Now, they will rise even more, especially for bread, wine, and fodder for horses. Already throughout Rome one suffers greatly from [the lack] of bread, because there is no flour and no way to grind, since all the mills are broken or flooded. So great is the disorder and confusion that I do not know how this [situation] will be remedied soon.

You should know that in Florence the Arno also flooded the land in the same way and caused great damage. Because of the similar effects, in addition to what we have learned these days, we can discuss how things should be in our own city [of Mantua] when the Po breaks its banks. When I think about this, it makes me feel deeply distressed and filled with worry. Still, let it please our Lord God that the damage shall not be as bad as I imagine.

❧ ❧

❧

BIBLIOGRAPHY

This edition is based on Luis Gómez, *De prodigiosis Tyberis Inundationibus ab orbe condito ad annum M.D.XXXI Commentarii.* Rome: Francesco Minizio Calvo, 1531.

≈

Aberth, John. *An Environmental History of the Middle Ages: The Crucible of Nature.* London: Routledge, 2013.

Abulafia, David, ed. *The French Descent into Renaissance Italy, 1494–1495: Antecedents and Effects.* Aldershot: Variorum, 1995.

Aicher, Peter J. *Guide to the Aqueducts of Ancient Rome.* Wauconda, IL: Bolchazy-Carducci, 1995.

Akopyan, Ovanes, and David Rosenthal, ed. *Disaster in the Early Modern World: Examinations, Representations, Interventions.* Abingdon: Routledge, forthcoming.

Alberigo, Giuseppe. *I vescovi italiani al Concilio di Trento, 1545–1547.* Florence: G. C. Sansoni, 1959.

—. "Aleandro, Girolamo," DBI 2 (1960): 129–35.

Alberti, Leon Battista. *L'Architettura [De re aedificatoria].* 2 vols. Giovanni Orlandi, trans. Paolo Portoghesi, intro. and notes. Milan: Edizione il Polifilo, 1966.

—. *On the Art of Building in Ten Books.* Joseph Rykwert, Neil Leach, and Robert Tavernor, trans. Cambridge, MA: MIT Press, 1988.

Aldrete, Gregory S. *Floods of the Tiber in Ancient Rome.* Baltimore: Johns Hopkins University Press, 2007.

Alföldy, Géza. *Der Obelisk auf dem Petersplatz in Rom: Ein historische Monument der Antike.* Heidelberg: Carl Winter, 1990.

Andretta, Elisa. "Les médecins du Tibre: La construction d'un savoir sur les fleuves dans la Rome du 16e siècle." *Histoire, Médecine et Santé* 11 (2017): 99–129.

Annius of Viterbo, O.P., ed. *Berosus Babilonicus De his quae praecesserunt inundationem terrarum. Item, Myrsilus de origine Tyrrhenorum. Cato in fragmentis. Archilocus in Epitheto de temporibus. Metasthenes de iudicio temporum. Philo in breviario temporum. Xenophon de equiuocis temporum. Sempronius de divisione Italiae. Q. Fab. Pictor de aureo saeculo & origine [sic] urbis Rhomae. Fragmentum Itinerarii Antonini Pii. Altercatio Adriani Augusti & Epictici. Cornelii Taciti de origine & situ Germanorum opusculum. C.C. de situ & moribus Germanorum.* Paris: n.p., 1511.

Anonymous, *Diluvio di Roma che fu a VII d'ottobre, l'anno M.D. XXX... con ordinata discrittione di parte in parte.* Benvenuto Gasparoni, ed. *Arti e Lettere: Scritti Raccolti da Francesco e Benvenuto Gasparoni.* 2 vols. Rome: Tipografia delle Scienze Matematiche e Fisiche, 1865, 2:81–98, 106–31.

Arce, Javier. "El inventario di Roma: *Curiosum y Notitia.*" In *The Transformations of* Urbs Roma *in Late Antiquity.* W.V. Harris, ed. *Journal of Roman Archaeology.* Supplementary Series Number 33 (1999): 15–22.

Ascarelli, Fernanda. *La tipografia cinquecentina italiana.* Florence: Sansoni Antiquariato, 1953.

Bacci, Andrea. *Del Tevere: Della natura et bontà dell'acque & delle inondationi Libri II.* Rome: Vincenzo Luchino, 1558.

—. *Del Tevere [...] libri tre [...].* Venice: Aldus, 1576.

—. *Del Tevere dell'eccell. dottore medico e filosofo Andrea Baccio libro quarto.* Rome: Stampatori Camerali, 1599.

Barberi, Francesco. "Le edizioni romane di Francesco Minizio Calvo." In *Miscellanea di scritti di bibliografia ed erudizione in memoria di Luigi Ferrari.* Florence: L.S. Olschki, 1952, 57–97.

Bariviera, Chiara. "Region XI Circus Maximus." In Carandini and Carafa, 1:421–25.

Barnett, Lydia. *After the Flood: Imagining the Global Environment in Early Modern Europe.* Baltimore: Johns Hopkins University Press, 2019.

Bell, Robert E. *Women of Classical Mythology: A Biographical Dictionary.* Oxford: Oxford University Press, 1993.

Bencivenga, Mauro, Eugenio Di Loreto, Lorenzo Liperi. "Piene storiche del Tevere a Roma." *L'Acqua* 3 (1999): 17–24.

Beneyto, Juan. "Luis Gómez, jurista de Orihuela." *Anales del Centro de Cultura Valenciana,* 2d ser. 20 (1952): 192–95.

Benzoni, Gino. "Federico II Gonzaga, duca di Mantova e marchese del Monferrato." DBI 45 (1995): 710–22.

Bersani, Pio, and Mauro Bencivenga. *Le piene del Tevere a Roma dal V secolo a.C. all'anno 2000.* Rome: Servizio Idrografico e Mareografico Nazionale, 2010.

Bettini, Maurizio. "Vertumnus: A God with no Identity." *I Quaderni del Ramo d'Oro On Line* 3 (2010): 320–34.

Biancofiore, Angela. *Benvenuto Cellini artiste–écrivain: L'homme à l'oeuvre.* Paris: Harmattan, 1998.

Boccaccio, Giovanni. *Genealogiae Joannis Boccatii cum demonstrationibus in formis arborum designatis eiusdem de montibus [et] sylvis, de fontibus, lacubus [et] fluminibus ac etiam de stagnis [et] paludibus, necnon [et] de maribus, seu diversis maris nominibus.* Venice: Agostino Zani, 1511.

—. *Genealogy of the Pagan Gods.* John Solomon, ed. and trans. 2 vols. Cambridge, MA: Harvard University Press, 2011–17.

Bonaccorso, Giuseppe. "Roma e le sue acque potabili nel Cinquecento: La competizione con il Tevere." *Roma Moderna e Contemporanea* 17 (2009): 73–90.

Bracke, Wouter. *Fare la epistola nella Roma del Quattrocento.* Rome: Roma nel Rinascimento, 1992.

Brentano, Robert. *Rome Before Avignon: A Social History of Thirteenth–Century Rome.* New York: Basic Books, 1974.

Brezzi, Paolo. *Roma e l'impero medioevale (774–1252).* Storia di Roma 10. Bologna: Licinio Cappelli, 1947.

Brunelli, Giampiero. "Grimani, Marino." DBI 59 (2002): 640–46.

Buzzetti, Carlo. "Portus Tiberinus." LTUR 4:155–56.

—, and Giuseppina Pisani Sartorio. "Clivus Argentarius." LTUR 1:280.

Byatt, Lucinda. "Ridolfi, Niccolò." DBI 87 (2016): 471–75.

Camesasca, Ettore, and Nino Borsellino. "Cellini, Benvenuto." DBI 23 (1979): 440–51.

Capitani, Ovidio. "Gregorio IX." DBI 59 (2002): 166–78.

Carafa, Paolo, and Paola Pacchiarotti. "Region XIV Transtiberim." In Carandini and Carafa, 1:549–82.

Carandini, Andrea, and Paolo Carafa, ed. *Atlas of Ancient Rome: Biography and Portraits of the City.* 2 vols. Andrew Campbell Halavais, trans. Princeton, NJ: Princeton University Press, 2017.

Carcani, Michele. *Il Tevere: Le sue inondazioni dall'origine di Roma fino ai giorni nostri*. Rome: Tipografia Romana, 1875.

Cassiani, Chiara, and Myriam Chiabò, ed. *Pomponio Leto e la prima accademia romana*. Rome: Roma nel Rinascimento, 2007.

Cassiodorus, *Variae*. Theodor Mommsen, ed. MGH, *Auctores Antiquissimi* 12. Berlin: Weidman, 1894.

Castagnoli, Ferdinando. *Il Vaticano nell'antichità classica*. Vatican City: Biblioteca Apostolica Vaticana, 1992.

Castiglione, Giacomo. *Trattato dell'inondatione del Tevere di Iacomo Castiglione Romano*. Rome: Guglielmo Facciotto, 1599.

Cazzola, Franco. "Le bonifiche cinquecentesche nella valle del Po: Governare le acque, creare nuove terre." In *Arte e scienza delle acque nel Rinascimento*. Alessandra Fiocca, Daniela Lamberini, and Cesare Maffioli, ed. Venice: Marsilio, 2004, 15–35.

Cellini, Benvenuto. *Vita di Benvenuto Cellini*. Orazio Bacci, ed. Florence: Sansoni, 1901.

Chamberlain, E.W. *The Sack of Rome 1527*. New York: Dorset, 1979.

Chastagnol, André. "Les régionnaires de Rome." In *Les littératures techniques dans l'antiquité romaine: Statut, public et destination, tradition*. Claude Nicolet, ed. Geneva: Foundation Hardt, 1996, 179–97.

Chastel, André. *The Sack of Rome, 1527*. Beth Archer, trans. Princeton, NJ: Princeton University Press, 1983.

Cicconi, Maurizia. "E il papa cambiò strada: Giulio II e Roma. Un nuovo documento sulla fondazione di via Giulia." *Römisches Jahrbuch der Bibliotheca Hertziana* 41 (2013/14): 227–59.

Coarelli, Filippo. "Pons Aemilius." LTUR 4:106–7.

—. "Pons Agrippae, Pons Aurelius, Pons Valentiniani." LTUR 4:107–8.

—. "Pons Sublicius." LTUR 4:113.

Coffin, David R. *Gardens and Gardening in Papal Rome*. Princeton, NJ: Princeton University Press, 1991.

Conforti, Claudia. "Il cantiere di Michelangelo al Ponte Santa Maria a Roma (1548–49)." In *I ponti delle capitali d'Europa dal Corno d'Oro alla Senna*. Donatella Calabi and Claudia Conforti, ed. Milan: Electa, 2002, 75–87.

Cooley, Alison E. *The Cambridge Manual of Latin Epigraphy*. Cambridge: Cambridge University Press, 2012.

Curran, Brian A., Anthony Grafton, Pamela O. Long, and Benjamin Weiss. *Obelisk: A History*. Cambridge, MA: Burndy Library and MIT Press, 2009.

Dati, Giuliano. *Del diluvio de Roma del MCCCCXCV a dì IIII de decembre*. Anna Esposito and Paola Farenga, ed. Rome: Roma nel Rinascimento, 2011.

De Caprariis, Francesca. "Pons Aelius." LTUR 4:105–6.

De Cubellis, Mary. "Palazzo Falconieri a via Giulia: Contributi alla conoscenza della fortuna dell'edilizia privata di Francesco Borromini." MA diss., Università degli Studi di Roma "Tor Vergata," 2015/2016.

Del Re, Niccolò. *La Curia Capitolina e tre altri organi giudiziari romani*. Rome: Fondazione Marco Besso, 1993.

Dibner, Bern. *Moving the Obelisks*. Norwalk, CT: Burndy Library, 1950, repr. 1991.

Di Martino, Vittorio, Roswitha Di Martino, and Massimo Belati. *Huc Tiber Ascendit: Le memorie delle inondazioni del Tevere a Roma*. Rome: Arbor Sapientiae, 2017.

Di Paolo, Silvia. "Da regulae particolari a norme generali: Verso un diritto amministrativo della Chiesa (XV–XVI sec.)." *Historia et Ius* 11 (2017). Paper 6. At: www.historiaetius.eu.

D'Onofrio, Cesare. *Gli obelischi di Roma: Storia e urbanistica di una città dall'età antica al XX secolo*. 3rd ed. Rome: Romana Società Editrice, 1992.

—. *Il Tevere: L'Isola Tiberina, le inondazioni, i molini, i porti, le rive, i muraglioni, i ponti di Roma*. Rome: Romana Società Editrice, 1980.

Du Rivail, Aymar. *Civilis Historiae Iuris, sive in duodecim Tabularum Leges Commentariorum libri quinque*. Mainz: Schoeffer, 1527.

Duchesne, Louis, ed. *Liber Pontificalis*. 2 vols. Paris: Ernst Thorin, 1886.

Enzi, Silvia. "Le inondazioni del Tevere a Roma tra il XVI e XVIII secolo nelle fonti bibliotecarie del tempo." *Mélanges de l'École française de Rome, Italie et Méditerranée* 118.1 (2006): 13–20.

Esposito, Anna. "Il Tevere e Roma." In *La calamità ambientali nel tardo Medioevo europeo: Realtà, percezioni, reazioni*. Michael Matheus et al., ed. Florence: Firenze University Press, 2010, 257–75.

—. "Le inondazioni del Tevere tra tardo Medioevo e prima età moderna: Leggende, racconti, testimonianze." *Mélanges de l'École française de Rome, Italie et Méditerranée* 118.1 (2006): 7–12.

—. "Roma e i suoi 'diluvi.'" In Dati, *Del diluvio de Roma*, 5–26.

Esser, Raingard. "'Ofter gheen water op en hadde gheweest': Narratives of Resilience on the Dutch Coast in the Seventeenth Century." *Dutch Crossing* 40 (2016): 97–107.

Fagan, Brian. *The Little Ice Age: How Climate Made History, 1300–1850*. New York: Basic Books, 2000.

Fane-Saunders, Peter. *Pliny the Elder and the Emergence of Renaissance Architecture*. New York: Cambridge University Press, 2016.

Folliet, Joseph. "Gómez Louis." In *Dictionnaire de droit canonique*. Raoul Naz, ed. Paris: Librairie Letouzey et Ané, 1953, 5, cols. 974–75.

Fosi, Irene. *Papal Justice: Subjects and Courts in the Papal State, 1500–1750*. Thomas V. Cohen, trans. Washington, DC: Catholic University Press, 2011.

Frommel, Christoph Luitpold. "Il palazzo di Giuliano Ceci, precursore di Palazzo Falconieri." In *Il Palazzo Falconieri e il palazzo barocco a Roma: Atti del Convegno indetto all'Accademia d'Ungheria in Roma, Rome 24–26 maggio 1995*. Gábor Hajnóczi and Csorba László, ed. Soveria Mannelli–Catanzaro: Rubbettino, 2009, 15–27.

Frosini, Pietro. *Il Tevere: Le inondazioni di Roma e i provvedimenti presi dal governo italiano per evitarle*. Rome: Accademia Nazionale dei Lincei, 1977.

Gallucci, Margaret A. *Benvenuto Cellini: Sexuality, Masculinity, and Artistic Identity in the Renaissance*. New York: Palgrave Macmillan, 2003.

—, and Paolo L. Rossi, ed. *Benvenuto Cellini: Sculptor, Goldsmith, Writer*. New York: Cambridge University Press, 2004.

García y García, A. "Gómez, Luis." In *Diccionario de Historia Eclesiastica de España*. Madrid: Instituto Enrique Flores, 1972, 2:1026.

Gattoni da Camogli, Maurizio. *Clemente VII e la geopolitica dello Stato Pontificio (1523–1534)*. Vatican City: Archivio Segreto Vaticano, 2002.

Genovese, Carmen, and Daniela Sinisi. Pro ornatu et publica utilitate: *L'attività della Congregazione cardinalizia super viis, pontibus et fontibus nella Roma di fine '500*. Rome: Gangemi, 2010.

Gherardi, Jacopo. "Il diario romano di Jacopo Gherardi." Enrico Carusi, ed. RIS 23.3. Città di Castello: S. Lapi, 1904.

Gouwens, Kenneth. *Remembering the Renaissance: Humanist Narratives of the Sack of Rome*. Leiden: Brill, 1998.

—, and Sheryl E. Reiss, ed. *The Pontificate of Clement VII: History, Politics, Culture*. Aldershot: Ashgate, 2005.

Grafton, Anthony. *Cardano's Cosmos: The Worlds and Works of a Renaissance Astrologer*. Cambridge, MA: Harvard University Press, 1999.

—. "Invention of Traditions and Traditions of Invention in Renaissance Europe: The Strange Case of Annius of Viterbo." In *The Transmission of Culture in Early Modern Europe*. Anthony Grafton and Ann Blair, ed. Philadelphia: University of Pennsylvania Press, 1990, 8–38.

Gregory of Tours. *Historiae Francorum*. Bruno Krusch and Wilhelm Levison, ed. MGH, *Scriptores Rerum Merovingicarum* 1. Hanover: Hahn, 1951.

Grove, Jean M. *Little Ice Ages: Ancient and Modern* 1. 2nd ed. London: Routledge, 2004.

Guainerio, Antonio. *De Peste*. Venice: Rinaldo da Nimega, 1540.

Guicciardini, Luigi. *The Sack of Rome*. James H. Mc Gregor, trans. New York: Italica Press, 1993.

Hainsworth, Peter, and David Robey, ed. *Oxford Companion to Italian Literature*. Oxford: Oxford University Press, 2002.

Hamill, Les. *Bridge Hydraulics*. Boca Raton: CRC Press, 1999.

Hansen, Morten Steen. "Rainbow and the Incarnation: Lotto, Correggio, and the Deluge of 1524." In *Lorenzo Lotto: Contesti, significati, conservazione*. Francesca Coltrinari and Enrico Maria Dal Pozzolo, ed. Ponzano Veneto: ZeL Edizioni, 2019, 206–25.

Herrero Mediavilla, Victor. ed. *Indice Biográfico de España, Portugal e Iberoamérica* (ADEPI). 4th ed. 7 vols. Munich: K.G. Saur, 2007.

Hook, Judith. *The Sack of Rome, 1527*. London: Macmillan, 1972.

Hornblower, Simon, Anthony Spawforth, and Esther Eidinow, ed. *The Oxford Classical Dictionary*, 4th ed. Oxford: Oxford University Press, 2012.

Hosie, Simon Alistair. "'Cataloguing the Empire': The Regionary Catalogues and the Role and Purpose of Bureaucratic Inventories." MPhil diss.: University of Sheffield, 2016.

Infessura, Stefano. *Diario della città di Roma*. Oreste Tommasini, ed. Rome: Forzani E.C. Tipografi del Senato, 1890.

Ishii, Teresa Robertson, and Philip Atkins. "Essential vs. Accidental Properties." *Stanford Encyclopedia of Philosophy*. At: https://plato.stanford.edu/entries/essential-accidental.

Istasse, Nathaël. "Joannes Ravisius Textor: Mise au point biographique." *Bibliothèque d'Humanisme et Renaissance* 69 (2007): 691–703.

—. "Le *Specimen Epithetorum* (1518) et le *Epitheta* (1524): J Ravisius Textor compilateur et créateur." In *L'épithète, la rime et la raison: La lexicographie poétique en Europe, XVIe–XVIIe siècles*. S. Hache and A.-P. Pouey-Mounou, ed. Paris: Classiques Garniers, 2015, 79–121.

Iversen, Erik. *Obelisks in Exile* 1. *The Obelisks of Rome*. Copenhagen: GEC Gad, 1968.

Jacks, Philip. *The Antiquarian and the Myth of Antiquity: The Origins of Rome in Renaissance Thought*. Cambridge: Cambridge University Press, 1993.

Jacobus de Voragine. *Legenda Aurea*. Alessandro Brovarone and Lucetta Vitale Brovarone, ed. Milan: Einaudi, 2007.

—. *The Golden Legend: Readings on the Saints*. William Granger Ryan, trans. 1. Princeton, NJ: Princeton University Press, 1993.

Janku, Andrea, Gerrit J. Schenk, and Franz Mauelshagen, ed. *Historical Disasters in Context: Science, Religion, and Politics*. New York: Routledge, 2012.

Juvenal. *Satirae cum commentis Antonii Mancinelli, Domitii Calderini, Georgii Vallae*. Nuremberg: Anton Koberger, 1497.

Karmon, David. *Ruin of the Eternal City: Antiquity and Preservation in Renaissance Rome*. New York: Oxford University Press, 2011.

Koller, Alexander. "Lippomano, Luigi (Aloisio, Alvise)." DBI 65 (2005): 243–46.

Lee, Egmont, ed. Habitatores in Urbe: *The Population of Renaissance Rome/La popolazione di Roma nel Rinascimento*. Rome: Casa Editrice Università La Sapienza, 2006.

Leguay, Jean-Pierre. *L'air et le vent au Moyen Âge*. Rennes: Presses Universitaires de Rennes, 2011.

Leto, Giulio Pomponio. *De romanae Urbis vestustate noviter impressus*. Rome: Giacomo Mazzocchi, 1515.

Leveau, Philippe. "Mentalité économique et grands travaux: Le drainage du Lac Fucin aux origines d'un modèle." *Annales ESC* 48 (1993): 3–36.

Ligota, Christopher R. "Annius of Viterbo and His Historical Method." *Journal of the Warburg and Courtauld Institutes* 50 (1987): 44–57.

Liverani, Paolo. *La topografia antica del Vaticano*. Vatican City: Monumenti, Musei e Gallerie Pontificie, 1999.

—. "Pons Neronianus." LTUR 4:111.

Logan, Oliver. *The Venetian Upper Clergy in the 16th and Early 17th Centuries: A Study in Religious Culture*. 2 vols. Salzburg: Institut für Anglistik und Amerikanistik Universität Salzburg, 1995.

Lonardi, Anna. *La cura riparum et alvei Tiberis: Storiografia, prosopografia e fonti epigrafiche*. BAR International Series 2464. Oxford: BAR Publishing, 2013.

Long, Pamela O. *Engineering the Eternal City: Infrastructure, Topography, and the Culture of Knowledge in Late Sixteenth-Century Rome*. Chicago: University of Chicago Press, 2018.

—. "Responses to a Recurrent Disaster: Flood Writings in Rome, 1476–1606." In *Disaster in the Early Modern World: Examinations, Representations, Interventions*. Ovanes Akopyan and David Rosenthal, ed. Abingdon: Routledge, forthcoming.

Macfarlane, Robert. *Underland: A Deep Time Journey*. New York: W.W. Norton, 2020.

Malipiero, Domenico, ed. *Annali Veneti Dall'Anno 1457 al 1500 ordinati e abbreviati dal Senatore Francesco Longo*. Florence: Gio. Pietro Vieusseax, 1848.

Marchus, Johannes. "Inondazioni a Roma, Venezia e Como nel 1478." *Bollettino Storico della Svizzera Italiana* 6 (1884): 107.

Marshall, David R. "Piranesi, Juvarra, and the Triumphal Bridge Tradition." *The Art Bulletin* 85.2 (2003): 321–52.

Marsico, Annalisa. *Il Tevere e Roma nell'alto medioevo: Alcuni aspetti del rapporto tra il fiume e la città*. Rome: Società alla Biblioteca Vallicelliana, 2018.

Martin, Craig. *Renaissance Meteorology: Pomponazzi to Descartes*. Baltimore: Johns Hopkins University Press, 2011.

McFarlane, I.D. "Reflections on Ravisius Textor's *Specimen Epithetorum*." In *Classical Influences on European Culture, A.D. 1500–1700*. R.R. Bolgar, ed. Cambridge: Cambridge University Press, 2010, 81–90.

Melchiorre, Matteo. "Sanudo, Marino il Giovane." DBI 90 (2017): 498–504.

Miglio, Massimo, et al., ed. *Il sacco di Roma del 1527 e l'immaginario collettivo*. Rome: Istituto Nazionale di Studi Romani, 1986.

Miranda, Salvador. "Aleandro, Girolamo (1480–1542)." In *The Cardinals of the Holy Roman Church*. At: https://cardinals.fiu.edu/bios1536. htm#Aleandro.

—. "Grimaldi, Girolamo (?–1543)." In *The Cardinals of the Holy Roman Church*. At: https://cardinals.fiu.edu/bios1527-ii.htm#Grimaldi.

—. "Loaysa y Mendozo, O.P., Garcia de (1478–1546)." In *The Cardinals of the Holy Roman Church*. At: https://cardinals.fiu.edu/bios1530. htm#Loaysa.

—. "Ridolfi, Niccolò (1501–1550)." In *The Cardinals of the Holy Roman Church*. At: https://cardinals.fiu.edu/bios1517-ii.htm#Ridolfi.

Modigliani, Anna. *Roma al tempo di Leon Battista Alberti (1432–1472)*. Rome: Roma nel Rinascimento, 2019.

Modio, Giovanni Battista. *Il Tevere*. Rome: Vincenzo Luchino, 1556.

Muecke, Frances. "Humanists in the Roman Forum." *Papers of the British School at Rome* 71 (2003): 207–33.

NASA Eclipse website. "Five Millennium Catalog of Lunar Eclipses." At: https://eclipse.gsfc.nasa.gov/LEcat5/LE1501-1600.html.

—. "Five Millennium Catalog of Solar Eclipses." At: https://eclipse.gsfc. nasa.gov/SEcat5/SE1501-1600.html.

Niccoli, Ottavia. "Il diluvio del 1524 fra panico collettivo e irrisione carnevalesca." In *Scienze, credenze occulte, livelli di cultura: Convegno internazionale di studi, Firenze, 26–30 giugno 1980*. Florence: L.S. Olschki, 1982, 369–92.

Nichols, Charlotte, and James H. Mc Gregor, ed. *Renaissance Naples: A Documentary History, 1400–1600.* New York: Italica Press, 2019.

Nordh, Arvast. *Libellus de regionibus urbis Romae.* Lund: C.W.K. Gleerup, 1949.

Omont, Henri, ed. "Journal autobiographique `du cardinal Jérôme Aléandre (1480–1530) publié d'après manuscrits de Paris et d'Udine." *Notices et extraits des manuscrits de la Bibliothèque Nationale et d'autres bibliothèques* 35 (1895): 2–115.

Palermino, Richard J. "The Roman Academy, the Catacombs and the Conspiracy of 1468." *Archivum Historiae Pontificiae* 18 (1980): 117–55.

Palmieri, Matteo. *Liber de Temporibus.* Gino Scaramella, ed. RIS 26.1. Città di Castello: S. Lapi, 1906–15.

Palombi, Domenico. "Regiones Quatturodecim (Topographia)." LTUR 4:199–204.

Paul the Deacon. *Historia Langobardoum.* L. Bethmann and G. Waitz, ed. MGH *Scriptores Rerum Langobardarum.* Hanover: Hahn, 1878.

Petroni, Alessandro T. *De victu romanorum et de sanitate tuenda libri quinque.* Rome: Stamperia del Popolo Romano, 1581.

Petrucci, Franca. "Cortesi, Tommaso." DBI 29 (1983): 772–73.

Piccolomini, Enea Silvio. *Epistolae familiares.* Milan: Ulrich Scinzenzeler, A. Archinto, J. Vinzalio, 1497.

Piccolomini, Iacopo Ammannati. *Lettere (1444–1479).* 3 vols. Paolo Cherubini, ed. Rome: Ministero per i Beni Culturali e Ambientali and Ufficio Centrale per i Beni Archivistici, 1997.

Pictor, Pseudo-Q. Fabius. *De aureo saeculo.* In Annius of Viterbo, ed. *Berosus Babilonicus De his quae praecesserunt inundationem terrarum.* Fol. XXIXv.

Pietrangeli, Carlo. *Guide Rionali di Roma. Rione VII: Regola.* Pt. 2. Rome: Fratelli Palombi, 1984.

Pignatti, Franco. "Una poetica inondazione: Francesco Maria Molza sull'alluvione di Roma del 7–8 Ottobre 1530 (e in morte di Clemente VII)." *Roma nel Rinascimento* (2017): 391–404.

Pisani Sartorio, Giuseppina. "Porta Flaminia." LTUR 3:303–4.

Platina, Bartolomeo. *Platynae historici Liber de vita Christi ac omnium pontificum; aa. 1–1474.* Giacinto Gaida, ed. RIS 3.1. Città di Castello: Scipione Lapi, 1913–32.

Ponsiglione, Giulia. *La "ruina" di Roma: Il sacco del 1527 e la memoria letteraria.* Rome: Carocci, 2010.

Prosperi, Adriano. "Clemente VII, papa." DBI 26 (1982): 237–59.

Ravisius Textor, Joannes. *Specimen epithetorum.* Paris: n.p., 1518.

Re, Emilio. "Maestri di Strada." *Archivio della R. Società Romana di Storia Patria* 43 (1920): 86–102.

"Repertorium Pomponianum." At: https://www.repertoriumpomponianum.it.

Riboullault, Denis. *Rome en ses jardins: Paysage et pouvoir au XVIe siècle.* Paris: CTHS/INHA, 2013.

Rike, R.L. Apex Omnium. *Religion in the Res Gestae of Ammianus.* Berkeley: University of California Press, 1987.

Rinne, Katherine Wentworth. *The Waters of Rome: Aqueducts, Fountains, and the Birth of the Baroque City.* New Haven: Yale University Press, 2010.

Riva di San Nazarro, Gianfrancesco. *Tractatus de Peste.* Lyons: Jacques Saccon, 1522.

Rolevinck, Werner. *Fasciculus temporum omnes antiquorum cronicas complectens.* Strasbourg: Johan Prüss [not before 1490].

Rowland, Ingrid D. *The Culture of the High Renaissance: Ancients and Moderns in Sixteenth-Century Rome.* Cambridge: Cambridge University Press, 1998.

Sabellico, Marcantonio. *Posterior pars eiusdem Rapsodie historiaru[m] M. Antonii Coccij Sabellici contine[n]s sex Enneades reliquas cu[m] earunde[m] repertorijs et epitomis.* Paris: Jehan Petit, 1513.

Salamito, Jean-Marie. "Pons Fabricius." LTUR 4:109–10.

Salerno, Luigi, Luigi Spezzaferro, and Manfredo Tafuri. *Via Giulia: Una utopia urbanistica del 500.* Rome: Aristide Staderini, 1973.

Sanga, Giovanni Battista. "Al Duca Alessandro de' Medici." In *Lettere di Principi le quali si scrivono o ai principi o ragionano di principi.* Venice: Giordano Zirletti, 1577, 3:114r–115r.

Sansa, Renato. "L'odore del contagio: Ambiente urbano e prevenzione delle epidemie nella prima età moderna." *Medicina e Storia* 2 (2002): 83–108.

Sanuto, Marino. *I Diarii di Marino Sanuto.* Guglielmo Berechet, Nicolò Barozzi, and Marco Allegri, ed. 54. Venice: Fratelli Visentini, 1899.

Scalia, Giuseppe. "*Turbidus Tiber:* In margine ad alcune antiche epigrafi su inondazioni tiberine." In *Studi in onore di Leopoldo Sandri.* Rome: Ministero per i Beni Culturali e Ambientali 1950, 3:873–79.

Schraven, Minou. "Founding Rome Anew: Pope Sixtus IV and the Foundation of the Ponte Sisto, 1473." In *Foundation, Dedication, and Consecration in Early Modern Europe.* Maarten Delbeke and Minou Schraven, ed. London: Brill, 2012, 129–51.

Schwab, Maren Elisabeth, and Anthony Grafton. *The Art of Discovery: Digging into the Past in Renaissance Europe.* Princeton. NJ: Princeton University Press, 2022.

Scott, Russell T. "Domus Publica." LTUR 1:165–66.

—. "Regia." LTUR 4:189–92.

—. "Vesta, aedes." LTUR 5:125–28.

Sabellico, Marcantonio. *Posterior pars eiusdem Rapsodie historiaru[m] M. Antonio Coccij Sabellici contine[n]s sex Enneades reliquas cu[m] earunde[m] repertorijs et epitomis.* Paris: Jehan Petit, 1513.

Segarra Lagunes, Maria Margarita. *Il Tevere e Roma: Storia di una simbiosi.* Rome: Gangemi, 2004.

Setton, Kenneth M. *The Papacy and the Levant, 1204–1571.* 4 vols. Philadelphia, PA: American Philosophical Society, 1976–84.

Shaw, Christine, and Michael Mallett. *The Italian Wars, 1494–1559.* 2nd rev. ed. New York: Routledge, 2018.

Simoncini, Giorgio. *Roma: Le trasformazioni urbane nel Cinquecento 1. Topografia e urbanistica da Giulio II a Clemente VIII.* Florence: L.S. Olschki, 2008.

Simonetta, Marcello. "Sanga, Giovan Battista." DBI 90 (2017): 182–83.

Siraisi, Nancy G. "*Historiae*: Natural History, Roman Antiquity, and Some Roman Physicians." In *Historia: Empiricism and Erudition in Early Modern Europe.* Gianna Pomata and Nancy G. Siraisi, ed. Cambridge, MA: MIT Press, 2005, 325–54.

Smith, Leonard. "Pier Paolo Vergerio: *De Situ Veteris et Inclyte Urbis Rome.*" *The English Historical Review* 41 (1926): 571–77.

Spataro, Alberto, ed. Velud fulgor meridianus: *La 'Vita' di Papa Gregorio IX: Edizione, traduzione, commento.* Ordines 8. Milan: Vita e Pensiero, 2018.

Stephens, Walter. "When Pope Noah Ruled the Etruscans: Annius of Viterbo and His Forged 'Antiquities.'" Studia Humanitatis: *Essays in Honor of Salvatore Camporeale.* MLN. Italian Issue Supplement 119 (2004): S201–23.

Tafuri, Manfredo. "*Roma coda mundi:* The Sack of Rome: Rupture and Continuity." In Tafuri, *Interpreting the Renaissance: Princes, Cities, Architects.* Daniel Sherer, trans. New Haven: Yale University Press and Cambridge, MA: Harvard University Graduate School of Design, 2006, 157–59.

Taylor, Rabun. *Public Needs and Private Pleasures: Water Distribution, the Tiber River, and the Urban Development of Ancient Rome.* Rome: L'"Erma" di Bretschneider, 2000.

—. "Tiber River Bridges and the Development of the Ancient City of Rome." *The Waters of Rome*, 2 (June 2002): 3–4. At: https://waters.iath.virginia.edu/first.html.

Temple, Nicholas. Renovatio Urbis: *Architecture, Urbanism and Ceremony in the Rome of Julius II.* London: Routledge, 2011.

Tortelli, Giovanni. *Ioannis Tortelii Aretini orthographia. Ioannis Tortelii Lima quædam per Georgium Vallam tractatum de orthographia.* Venice: Tacuino, 1495.

Trebbi, Giuseppe. "Surian, Antonio." DBI 94 (2019): 541–44.

Turci, Marcello. "The Aqueducts." In Carandini and Carafa, 1:92–100.

Ugolini, Federico. *Visualizing Harbours in the Classical World: Iconography and Representation around the Mediterranean.* London: Bloomsbury, 2020.

Valentini, Roberto, and Giuseppe Zucchetti, ed. *Codice Topografico della città di Roma.* 4 vols. Rome: Tipografia del Senato, 1940–53.

Valeri, Elena. "Palmieri, Matteo." DBI 80 (2014): 614–18.

Virgili, Paola. "Vicus Iugarius." LTUR 5:169–70.

Victor, Publius, Pomponio Leto, Fabrizio Varano, Flavio Biondo, *De urbe Roma scribentes*. Flavio Biondo. *De locis ac civitatibus Italiae, deque eius appellationibus priscis ac novis*. Bologna: Girolamo Benedetti, 1520.

Vischer, Wilhelm, and Heinrich Boos, ed. "Johannis Knebel capellani ecclesie Basiliensis Diarium." *Basler Chroniken* 2 (1880): 408–9.

Viscogliosi, Alessandro. "Circus Flaminius." LTUR 1:269–72.

Vuković, Krešimir. "The Topography of the Lupercalia." *Papers of the British School at Rome* 86 (2018): 37–60.

Weil, Mark. *The History and Decoration of the Ponte S. Angelo*. University Park: Pennsylvania State University Press, 1974.

Wiseman, Timothy Peter. "Walls, Gates and Stories: Detecting Rome's Riverside Defences." *Papers of the British School at Rome* 89 (2021): 9–40.

Witcombe, Christopher L.C.E. *Copyright in the Renaissance: Prints and the Privilegio in Sixteenth-Century Venice and Rome*. Leiden: Brill, 2004.

—. *Print Publishing in Sixteenth-Century Rome: Growth and Expansion, Rivalry and Murder*. London: Harvey Miller/Brepols, 2008.

Zuccaro, Andrea. "Alcune osservazioni storiche e lessicali sull'editto del legato tiberiano Sotidius Libuscidianus (AE 1976, 653)." *Studi Classici e Orientali* 65.1 (2019): 245–75.

➳ ➳

➳

INDEX

ꝫ   ꝫ

ꝫ

Production of This Book Was Completed
on 10 June 2023 at Italica Press in
Clifton, Bristol, United Kingdom.
It Was Set in Adobe Jenson Pro
and MS Gothic Dingbats and
Printed on 55-Pound
Natural Paper.
꩜ ꩜ ꩜
꩜ ꩜
꩜

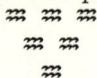